SNOW
LEOPARD

Snow Leopard

*How Legendary Writers Create
A Category Of One*

First published by Category Pirates 2022
Copyright © 2022 by Category Pirates

Category Pirates, Christopher Lochhead, Eddie Yoon, and Nicolas Cole assert the moral right to be identified as the authors of this work.

Category Pirates has no responsibility for the persistence or accuracy of URLs for external or third-party Internet Websites referred to in this publication and does not guarantee that any content on such Websites is, or will remain, accurate or appropriate.

Cover design by Zoe Norvell
Book design by I Need a Book Interior

First edition
ISBN: 978-1-956934-45-8

Writers without niches are "starving artists."

Writers with niches are Category Kings.

TABLE OF CONTENTS

Introduction

Legendary writers, the ones who stand the test of time, create a category of one.

They're snow leopards.

Regular leopards, the ones with golden fur and black spots, spend their entire lives competing against each other. They look the same. They act the same. They move in groups. They seek acceptance. The snow leopard does none of these things. In fact, it's rare to see even two snow leopards together. Ever.

They stand alone.

Most writers, communicators, creators, and leaders in every industry spend their entire lives trying to be the best "regular leopard" they can be. They believe their goal is to be the fastest, or the smartest, or the most cunning one in the pack. But no matter how fast, savvy, or smart they become, they're still just a regular leopard—one of many. They're stuck playing the "better" game, and the value of their existence sits in the context of their competition.

The big secret to becoming a legendary writer, creator, entrepreneur, or builder in the world is that your goal is not to play the "better" game and strive to be a newer, faster, smarter version of what everyone else is (a leopard). Your goal is to be a DIFFERENT type of writer altogether.

Your goal is to become a snow leopard.

And to dominate your category of one.

CHAPTER ONE

The Content Pyramid

The 5 Levels Of Becoming A Legendary Writer, Creator, and Thought Leader

Everyone today wants to be a thought leader.

They want to be seen as forward thinking. They want to be celebrated as the guru, the expert, The All Knowing One of their industry. They want to be the keynote speaker, the best-selling author, the person listed in the next "10 Marketers To Watch In 2022" *Forbes* article (most of which are paid placements, *just so you know*). Because now that the world has gotten exposed to the power of digital "attention," and everyone believes "the most valuable thing you could possibly have is an audience," well, everyone wants one for themselves.

Unfortunately, as we wrote about in *The "Me" Disease*, the vast majority of people who want to be a "thought leader" or best-selling author in today's digital, gamified world **don't have any leading thoughts.** That is to say: they are not actually contributing new, differentiated ideas. What they want is to be "seen" as a thought leader—to collect badges of approval and amass "followers" and social metrics that send the signal that lots of other people say they are important—without having to say anything unique, meaningful, or different. More importantly, they want "the audience" without having to take the time to think deeply about who they are creating for and why.

They want the outcome without the process.

And since this has become such a desirable goal, there are now strategies for shortcutting your way to instant "status" gratification.

The key is to cater to the lowest common denominator.

The way the business world has been educated on how to become an overnight "thought leader" is to create content that doesn't threaten, doesn't challenge, and doesn't require the audience to think—as loud and as often as possible.

This strategy caters to lazy, button-smashing consumers. When these people scroll through their social media feeds, they are (usually) not looking to be challenged.

Instead, they are in a state of searching for confirmation bias.

- "It takes every single person in the organization to achieve what you want to achieve." **Duh. Yes. Like.**
- "Authenticity is crucial to creating content that resonates." **For sure. Got it. Comment.**
- "If you want to change the world, you have to change yourself." **Totally. I'm a world-changer too. Share.**

Which is why the most viral content caters to lowest common denominator emotions: rage, joy, wonder, sadness, shock, surprise, desire, and so on.

As a result, most people do not define "being a thought leader" as having something unique and different to say. The way the world defines a "thought leader" (especially the digital world) is by measures of public approval. **It's a video game.** How many followers do you have? How many views does your content get? How many subscribers are on your email list? How many books have you sold? How many keynote speeches have you given? How many *Forbes* articles have called you an "expert?" How many recognizable names say you're important?

And since this game is largely about external signals of credibility, it makes sense why so many smart, well-intentioned, successful people decide to optimize for the path of least resistance. Out of nowhere, they start posting BGOs (Blinding Glimpses of the Obvious) because this sort of non-threatening content is the easiest way to get Likes and climb the perceived ladder of success without ruffling any feathers.

We call this content-free content.

It gets Likes and Views. It lands you some followers. But after you (the consumer) eat it, you sort of feel like you ate a box full of Oreos.

Zero nutritional value, full of empty calories, and left feeling stupid.

For those who don't want to cater to the lowest common denominator, but still don't have anything valuable to say, the other strategy is to add complexity to sound "smart."

This is how most academics and consultants approach thought leadership.

For example, *Reengineering The Corporation* by James Champy and Michael Hammer was a seminal business book and management idea. It kicked off an entire subsector of management consulting that generated hundreds of millions of dollars in fees and made CSC Index "the bell of the ball" among consulting firms for a brief period during the '80s and '90s.

Engineering a business sounds very technical and complicated. This was intentional by design—to scare clients into thinking they needed help.

Yet the core ideas were very simple:
- If any business process/activity doesn't add value to the customer, get rid of it.
- Redesign every business process to cut costs, especially via technology/automation.

But isn't this what companies are supposed to do anyways in the normal course of doing business?

The truth is, ideas like these are easy to understand but hard to execute. And since simplicity doesn't sell services, many academics and consultants complicate the language to make a simple idea feel like rocket science to justify their fees to come in and do the work.

We wouldn't classify this "languaging" as much as anti-languaging, which is the art of making up new words and acronyms for simple ideas that sound equally appealing and intimidating at the same time.

Thought Leadership 101

Listen to the words.

Thought. Leadership.

In order to be a "thought leader," you must be willing to LEAD WITH YOUR THOUGHTS.

This means it is your responsibility to say things people have not said yet. It is your responsibility to take risks, challenge conventional wisdom, and (dare we say) allow yourself to be creative—not in the art school "I'm-creative-just-like-you" way, but in the Elon Musk "I'm-going-to-Mars-F-U" sort of way. This is not about being outrageous or controversial for the sake of attention. It's about taking the world somewhere new *because you are already living in the future.*

And you're on a mission to get everyone else there with you.

The big question, "How?"

Anyone can say, "The key to creating content that resonates is to be authentic." The problem is, do you know what that means? How do we measure authenticity? What action step can you take after hearing that advice? (Most people come up empty-handed.)

So, we want to put a compass in your hands.

We've put together what we like to call The Content Pyramid.

The Content Pyramid: The 5 Levels Of Becoming A Legendary Writer, Creator, And Thought Leader

There are 5 levels to becoming a legendary writer, creator, and "thought leader" in your field.

- **Level 1:** Consumption
- **Level 2:** Curation
- **Level 3:** Obvious Connection
- **Level 4:** Non-Obvious Connection
- **Level 5:** Category Creation

Unfortunately, most people who aspire to be a "thought leader" (by any definition of the term) struggle to make it past Levels 2 or 3 on The Content Pyramid. They mistake passionately sharing someone else's ideas, or stating a "Blinding Glimpse of the Obvious," for thought leadership. Again, while this might be a terrific strategy for getting short-term Likes, Followers, and public approval, there is a giant difference between Gary Vaynerchuk and Nassim Nicholas Taleb. One contributes radically different, timeless thinking to modern society. The other bashes into your skull: "You just need to create content. Content, content, content."

It should be no surprise that Gary Vee's social media following completely dwarfs Nassim Nicholas Taleb's. (Stupid scales.)

Ask yourself: Do you want acceptance? Or do you want to make a difference?

Before we dive in, it's important to level-set your expectations.

If you want to be a legendary writer, creator, entrepreneur, executive, or industry thought leader, you need to be honest with yourself about a) how you measure success, and b) what category you're going to play in. For example, Nassim Nicholas Taleb, author of the best-selling book *The Black Swan*, writes about macroeconomics, mathematics, and statistics. He is brilliant, and has contributed significantly to humanity's understanding of "antifragile" systems. (His work was referenced profusely throughout the COVID-19 pandemic, as the pandemic revealed the "fragility" of our world.)

Gary Vaynerchuk, also a best-selling author, writes and speaks and creates content about happiness, success, business motivation, and creating content. No one has ever credited Gary Vee with changing the world in any meaningful way—however his audience is 15-25x larger than Nassim Nicholas Taleb's, and we'd bet he accumulates 1000x more exposure on his content than Taleb or any other modern thinker. (Mr. Vee also spends big money to go "viral," but that's a whole other conversation.)

And the reason why is very simple—and has much less to do with "marketing" than most people realize.

- **Nassim Nicholas Taleb** creates top-of-the-pyramid, differentiated, Non-Obvious content in smaller topic categories (macroeconomics, mathematics, and statistics).
- **Gary Vee** creates bottom-of-the-pyramid, undifferentiated, Obvious content in larger topic categories (happiness, success, business motivation, content creation).

The number one mistake aspiring writers, creators, and industry thought leaders make is wanting to have the impact of Taleb, but measuring success like Gary Vee. Do you think Nassim Nicholas Taleb cares how many Likes his post about "how at low variance the lognormal masquerades as a normal" gets? Of course not. He wants to have smart, Non-Obvious discussions about difficult, niche topics. Meanwhile, Gary Vee has an entire floor of his advertising agency solely dedicated to maximizing the reach & engagement of every one of his YouTube videos, LinkedIn posts, and Tweets—all of which say some variation of the same thing: "Success is all about perspective." *Oh, ok. Thx.*

So before you even start "playing the game" of writing and *leading with your thoughts*, you need to make a decision.

Do you want to make a difference? Then you need to divorce yourself from public approval. "Different" things don't get accepted right away. Meaningful things take time to understand. And Non-Obvious connections require people to think—and guess what? Most people scrolling through social media don't want to think.

Or, do you want to be accepted? If you want to be accepted, if you want lots of followers and engagement and badges that say you're awesome (in the short term), then Tweet, post, and make videos catering to the lowest common denominator. Parrot the same things everyone else says ("The key to success is hard work, determination, and grit!"). Don't threaten, don't challenge, and optimize for confirmation bias. The more you can create content people will engage with while their brain is turned off and they're borderline comatose, *scrolling, scrolling, scrolling,* the better.

People say they want the former, but drool over the latter.

The Size Of The Question Dictates The Size Of The Audience

The second thing you need to wrap your head around is: the category matters.

When you "create," you are creating something for someone. (Anyone who says, "Yea well, I just want to create for myself," is a beginner and

hasn't gotten far enough down the road to realize they aren't who matters—the reader, the listener, the viewer is who matters.)

That "someone" is your audience.

The question is, *how many people are in the audience?*

Better yet, *how many people could there be in the audience?*

What most writers, creators, and aspiring thought leaders do is they
sit down and decide they want to create or write something, first. Then,
once they're done, they go to work trying to get the whole world to pay
attention. (But remember: no one owes you their attention. And just
because you took the time to write it doesn't mean everyone else has to
take the time to read it.)

The problem is: the whole world might not be interested in what
you've made. Let's say you sat down and decided to write an essay about
the importance of owning a farm of chickens. Well, the only people who
are going to pay attention are the ones who woke up that morning with
that question. "You know what? I'd really like to know what it's like to
own a farm of chickens."

(Pirate Christopher has chickens, *aka little dinosaurs*, and thinks if
more people knew
how awesome they were, more people would have them.)

This is the value exchange that happens between every writer and
reader, creator and consumer, thought leader and "follower."

So, if you want to reach a lot of people, then you need to answer questions a lot of people have ("How can I make more money? How can I be
happier? How do I get promoted?"). Conversely, if you want to reach a
small number of people in a highly engaging way, then you need to answer
small, hyper-relevant questions only those types of people would be interested in ("How can I make more money as a middle school teacher? What
are jobs I can do as a stay-at-home mom with 2 kids working part-time?
What are some easy ways to remember the fundamentals of algebra?").

The size of the question dictates the size of the audience.

The reason so many aspiring thought leaders create Obvious, non-threatening content is because their goal isn't actually to "lead thoughts" in a different direction. Their goal is to increase the number next to their profile picture that says how many people on planet earth think they're awesome—so they can use that number to book speaking gigs, sell products, or just fall asleep a little bit easier at night knowing they're "Liked" online.

In fact, as a rule of thumb: people with giant audiences online tend to create the most surface-level, Obvious, content-free content.

Whereas the people with smaller, more niche audiences tend to create Non-Obvious, hyper-relevant content.

Consciously choosing which game you want to play is crucial to measuring your success as a writer, creator, entrepreneur, and thought leader.

Now, here's how to climb The Content Pyramid:

Level 1: Consumption

Internet culture has long called this The 1% Rule.

This means that on any given social media platform or website where users can participate, 1% of the users create the content, 9% of the users curate, organize, and update the content, and 90% of the users consume the content.

Most people spend their entire lives being content consumers—not content creators. And that's totally fine, so long as you understand you're not "playing the game." You're sitting on the sidelines watching the game.

In order to "get in the game," you must move out of consumption and up The Content Pyramid.

There are 2 types of "content consumers."

Passive (Lean Back) Consumers

These are people at the very bottom of The Content Pyramid who (typically) have an unconscious or even unhealthy relationship with media—in all its forms.

They spend day after day reading articles like "How To Get Rich," never putting their learnings into practice or taking any action. They watch motivational video after video, never leaving their couch. Or they cackle at TikToks of children getting hit in the face with large exercise balls well past their bedtime. The point is, they consume content that tends to over-promise and under-deliver. Especially in the business world, we call this content-free content. The more outrageous the claim in the headline, the more likely it is to be dumb and meaningless—and your life would be no different without it. As far as business content goes, *Inc Magazine* is the Category King here. "Elon Musk Does This 1 Thing Every Morning Before Breakfast" is a dumb headline. And, chances are, reading articles like this lead to no meaningful difference in your life.

The reason there is a place in the world for content like this is because, as we said, what most people consume is *content confirming things they already think*. They don't want new and different thoughts. They want the same thoughts parroted over and over and over again. (Which is why Gary Vee's content strategy works: just say things people want to hear and they'll keep smashing that Like button—like rats on cocaine.)

This is the equivalent of being intellectually morbidly obese, where you continue to consume empty intellectual calories until you realize your brain is so overweight you can't think for five minutes without needing a break to catch your breath.

Active (Lean Forward) Consumers

Making the transition from Passive to Active is the first step of climbing up The Content Pyramid.

This is "I choose to consume this" opposed to "Oh look, another shiny object!"

There's a terrific scene in *Crazy People* (a comedy from the '90s where an ad executive finds himself in a mental hospital) where ads are rewritten to be brutally honest to the consumer. Like a magazine spread that says: *"You may think phone service sucks since deregulation, but don't mess with us because we're all you got. In fact, if we fold, you'll have no damn phones. AT&T: We're tired of taking your crap."*

This is a bit like what happens as a consumer when you move from Passive to Active consumption. You understand that all content is a trade. You're aware of what you're buying (with your attention) and you're OK with the cost (time off your life). Some content you consume is extremely valuable, and other content you consume is mindless but makes you laugh. Either way, you are walking into the engagement with open eyes—and can tell when you're being sold something, tricked, or emotionally triggered.

But being conscious isn't the same as taking action and continuing to climb up The Content Ladder. So while you may be more aware than the chimpanzee next to you scrolling, scrolling, scrolling, at the end of the day, you're a consumer. (And that's ok, if that's what you want to do and how you want to spend your time.)

Level 2: Curation

Most people do not begin their journey as a writer, creator, or industry thought leader by creating original content.

Instead, they begin by imitating and curating thoughts, perspectives, insights, and ideas from people they admire. David Perell, internet writer & creator of *Write of Passage*, calls this "Imitate, then Innovate," which is the mental model many great creators over the ages have used to study those who came before them. They start by watching, learning, and internalizing the "rules," only to ultimately break them and forge a path of their own. Picasso studying Van Gogh's Impressionism and then a decade later moving on to create Cubism is a perfect example. (Every rock band starts off playing covers.)

There is nothing wrong with this strategy.

In fact, some people stay at Level 2 their entire lives, mastering the art of curating other people's ideas and never climbing further up The Content Pyramid. Tim Ferriss is probably the most well-known example of this, having created a career largely around organizing and distilling other people's insights opposed to sharing his own. And his podcast, as well as his best-selling books *Tools of Titans* or *Tribe of Mentors* show just how powerful intentional curation can be.

Ryan Holiday is another example of curation done well. Ryan Holiday's entire career isn't built on his own insights, but rather Marcus Auralius' insights and perspectives on Stoicism distilled and "made simple" for the modern reader. And *The Obstacle Is The Way* is a book of curated stories ("from John D. Rockefeller to Amelia Earhart to Ulysses S. Grant to Steve Jobs") to show those principles personified. There is nothing original about Ryan Holiday's work—and that's OK. He does great work. Curation is still a form of creation.

Intentional Curation

All of that said, curation is one of those skills that is very easy to learn and do but very difficult to master.

The lowest form of curation is Sharing. Like Retweeting someone else's content on Twitter. When you share someone else's content, *technically* you are being a curator. Of all the content out there, you're signaling "this thing" is important because you're sharing it from your profile.

Next is level of curation is adding your own opinion. You share something AND you tell the reader why you like it, don't like, feel happy or sad or upset or inspired by it. Communicating your own opinion on the content you are sharing makes you a creator. Because now the reader is consuming not just your judgment of the content you're curating but also consuming your perspective on the content.

Above that is curation with insight. Opinions are easy—everyone has one. But what's much more valuable than an opinion is an insight. This is what makes Ryan Holiday, Tim Ferriss, and other world-class curators so effective. Because even though they aren't the ones coming up with radically new and different ideas themselves, people read their work and listen to what they have to say because they trust their judgment, enjoy the thought leaders & content they curate, and appreciate hearing the insights they extract from the curated stories and perspectives.

This is how you start to move up The Content Pyramid.

Level 3: Obvious Connection

Whether you are curating other people's thoughts, insights, stories, and perspectives, or creating your own, the end result can be organized in two overarching mega categories.

- Obvious Connection
- Non-Obvious Connection

Gary Vaynerchuk creates Obvious Connections for his audience. His content is very linear and easy to understand. "You want to learn how to do content on social media? Here's how to create content on social media." A to B. One to two. Straight line.

Nassim Nicholas Taleb creates Non-Obvious Connections for his audience. His content is not linear. It's abstract, and requires drawing connections between seemingly unrelated data points. "Why do uncertain, improbable, 'Black Swan' events happen in modern society? Well, first, we need to understand the idea of robustness, which reflects an attitude where nothing is permitted to fail under conditions of change." A to Q. Five to Zebra. Curvy, chaotic, non-linear line. (Stuff that makes you think.)

When people move from Curator to Creator, they typically move into Obvious Connection first.

They have a topic and an audience in mind, and their goal is to move the audience from A to B:

- "Want to learn how to run Facebook ads? I'm going to teach you how to run Facebook ads."
- "Want to become financially independent? I'm going to show you how to become financially independent."
- "Want to trade stocks? I'm going to show you how to trade stocks."
- "Want to get promoted? I'm going to give you a 3-step process to get promoted."

Obvious Connection content is simple by design. Its goal is less esoteric, more actionable, and engineered to move readers incrementally forward in some meaningful way. To be clear: there is nothing wrong with this. Some of our favorite books, podcasts, and YouTube channels create absolutely terrific Obvious Connection content. The world needs it. We just want to make you conscious of the fact that Obvious Connections are incremental, whereas Non-Obvious Connections tend to be more rare, differentiated, and exponential.

The Benefits Of Drawing Obvious Connections

Obvious Connections have a short shelf life. *They matter right now.*

"This moved me forward in three steps." Non-Obvious Connections stand the test of time. They matter now and way in the future. "This changed my life." More importantly, most Non-Obvious Connections tend to gain in value over time as more and more people "get" it.

If you are a writer, creator, entrepreneur, or industry leader who wants to start building an audience, category and customer base, and monetize your knowledge and expertise in the short term, the fastest path to these outcomes is creating Obvious Connections. **Think of this as Demand Capture vs Demand Creation.** When you are drawing an Obvious Connection, the person already understands what you're talking about—and all you're doing is moving them forward. (Aka: the "market" in the person's mind already exists.) When you're drawing a Non-Obvious Connection, the person likely doesn't understand what you're talking about at first—which means you need to first give them a bunch of context they don't have, and then walk them around your thinking a few times before they "get it." (Aka: the "market" in the person's mind doesn't exist *yet*. You have to build it for them.)

From a thought leadership perspective, if your goal is to get attention and money quickly, it's typically much easier to do so by incrementally moving someone forward three steps opposed to picking them up and planting them in a new universe. Non-Obvious Connections require them to think—and remember, most people don't want to "think." They just want to Like and Comment on stuff they already think and agree with. (Today what most people call "thinking" is actually the mental Retweeting of an idea they already Like and agree with. *And that is the furthest thing from thinking.*)

So, the pro of creating Obvious Connections for your readers is more immediate, and dare we say more "guaranteed" acceptance and approval. There's nothing threatening about you telling people: "I will teach you how to close more sales leads, faster."

The con of creating Obvious Connections for your reader is that, without some intentional category design & languaging, you are most likely just a slightly better version of the person (or company) who came before you, and there's almost nothing about what you're creating that is defensible against the person who comes after you. You're easily replaceable. You're a content creator on a hamster wheel. Because what happens when the next Obvious Connector comes along and draws Obvious Connections even better than you? Then what? (You're stuck in the Better Trap.)

Level 4: Non-Obvious Connection

The same way there is a canyon-sized gap at the bottom of The Content Pyramid between Consumers and Curators (people who aren't "in the game" vs people who have thrown on a jersey and jumped onto the court), there is also a canyon-sized gap near the top of The Content Pyramid between Obvious Connectors and Non-Obvious Connectors.

It's the difference between *The Subtle Art of Not Giving A F*ck* and *Thinking, Fast and Slow.*

*The Subtle Art of Not Giving A F*ck* is one of the best-selling non-fiction books of the past decade and has sold over 10 million copies in just a few years (published 2016)—but will likely become irrelevant this decade.

Meanwhile, *Thinking, Fast and Slow* has sold a fraction of the amount (under 3 million copies) in double the length of time (published 2012), but is a book that will remain relevant well beyond any of our lifetimes, and shares radically new and different thinking discovered by author Daniel Kahneman, who won a Nobel Prize in Economics.

Which one do you want to be?

(There actually isn't a right or wrong answer to this question. It's just worth pointing out how many people say they want the latter, but manically refresh their social media metrics and sales data clearly obsessed with the former.)

Non-Obvious Connectors are writers, creators, entrepreneurs, and thought leaders who *change the world with their thinking.* The unfortunate part, however, is that data shows us most people don't want their thinking changed. They just want to be moved forward in some incremental way, and to be told things that validate (or remind them) of their current beliefs—which is why the top Non-Obvious Connectors universally sell far less copies, and receive far less attention on social media than Obvious Connectors.

We call this The Copernicus Dilemma.

In 1543, Nicolaus Copernicus hypothesized that the earth, along with the other planets, rotated around the sun. Up until this point (for nearly 1,000 years), Aristotle's view was that Earth was stationary and at the center of a revolving universe (which had become accepted as conventional wisdom). Everyone agreed, and anyone who didn't was considered crazy. When Nicolaus Copernicus finally published his theory, shortly before his death, almost no one took him seriously—and followers, like Italian scientist, Gioradno Bruno, were even burned at the stake for teaching such a thing.

It took more than a century for Copernicus' Non-Obvious Connection that the earth revolves around the sun, not the other way around, to become widely accepted.

Of course, we're still talking about Copernicus today, which is what makes Non-Obvious Connections such a dilemma. If you are the one going out on a limb and saying things no one has been willing to say *yet,* and/or connecting two disparate data points together to arrive at a new and highly different conclusion unaccepted by the status quo (the true definition of a "thought leader"), then you are most likely not going to receive immediate acclaim and approval. In fact, the opposite is more likely to happen: you will be ridiculed. You will be disavowed (and maybe even extradited from your home country). However, if and when the world comes around and is able to see things the way you see them, it's likely your point of view will stand the test of time.

So again: which one do you want?

Most people claim they want to change the world with their thinking, but really what they want is dinner party approval and instant gratification.

Examples of Non-Obvious Connectors

Malcolm Gladwell is a Non-Obvious Connector. He picks a topic, and then curates juxtaposing and surprising stories that, when held together, allow the reader to draw Non-Obvious Connections. His book *Talking To Strangers* is a great example of this, and the book's description is one giant signal of Non-Obvious Connection:

> *"How did Fidel Castro fool the CIA for a generation? Why did Neville Chamberlain think he could trust Adolf Hitler? Why are campus sexual assaults on the rise? Do television sitcoms teach us something about the way we relate to one another that isn't true?*
>
> *Talking to Strangers is a challenging and controversial excursion through history, psychology, and scandals taken straight from the news. In it, Malcolm Gladwell revisits the deceptions of Bernie Madoff, the suicide of Sylvia Plath, and the death of Sandra Bland—throwing our understanding of these and other stories into doubt."*

Freakonomics, written by Steven Levitt (Professor of Economics at the University of Chicago) and Stephen J. Dubner, is another timeless example of Non-Obvious Connections. Again, the answer as to whether a book, blog post, or piece of content is drawing an Obvious or Non-Obvious Connection is usually hidden in the title, description, or introduction. In the case of *Freakonomics*:

> *"Which is more dangerous, a gun or a swimming pool? Which should be feared more: snakes or french fries? Why do sumo wrestlers cheat? Dubner and Levitt present a brilliant—and brilliantly entertaining—account of how incentives of the most hidden sort drive behavior in ways that turn conventional wisdom on its head."*

Adam Grant (author of *Think Again*), Cal Newport (author of *Digital Minimalism*), Susan Cain (author of *Quiet*), these are authors who write books every few years, and when they finally hit publish it's to reveal a new, Non-Obvious Connection to readers. We see Non-Obvious content largely in the psychology category, however it's also hiding in plain sight in "less obvious" categories like relationships (*The 5 Love Languages*), personal development (*Becoming Supernatural*), as well as business & money (*The Changing World Order*).

Again, it's worth noting that while Non-Obvious Connections tend to have longer shelf lives, they also tend to sell less (and attract significantly less attention) than their Obvious counterparts. (Most new categories lean Non-Obvious... obviously!) Malcolm Gladwell's *Talking To Strangers* has sold a million copies, whereas Jen Sincero's *You Are A Badass* has sold more than 5 million.

It's not that one is "better" than the other.

It's that one draws Non-Obvious Connections whereas the other draws Obvious Connections.

And, especially in the near term, there is a much larger audience for Obvious content than there is for Non-Obvious content.

Level 5: Category Creation

The top of The Content Pyramid is Category Creation.

Both Obvious Connectors and Non-Obvious Connectors can achieve the top of the pyramid. Even curators (like Ryan Holiday or Tim Ferriss) can achieve the top of the pyramid. And that's because the highest level of creation is category creation—becoming known for a niche you own.

- Ryan Holiday dominates the category of Stoicism.
- James Clear dominates the category of habit-building.
- Jen Sincero dominates the category of "badass women."
- Nassim Nicholas Taleb dominates the category of probability.
- Category Pirates dominates the category of Category Design.

When you are first starting out as a writer, creator, or aspiring "thought leader," you think your goal is to hit a home run. You want to write a best-selling book. You want to go viral. You want to win an award.

It's not until you get going on your journey, and start climbing up The Content Pyramid, that you learn the flaws of your pursuit. Your goal isn't to write one great book—your goal is to write dozens, if not hundreds of great books. And your goal isn't to create one viral video— your goal is to create hundreds, maybe thousands of viral videos. As a result, your mindset shifts from being known as the creator of "one product" to being known for a unique and differentiated category. Ryan Holiday isn't known for just one book. He's known for all-things-Stoicism. And if you're a fan of Ryan Holiday, you don't want to just read *The Obstacle Is The Way*. You want to read more books, and watch more videos, and consume more content about the category of Stoicism. (This is why authors like Stephen King have such huge libraries. Readers keep coming back, again and again, because they're in love with the author's category. And they'll take as much as they can get.)

New Category, New Business Models

The benefit of creating your own category, and becoming known for a niche you own, isn't just radical differentiation.

You also unlock new business models for yourself.

When people are in love with your category, they don't just want one book. They want dozens of books *on the topic*. And they want courses going into depth on the topic. And they want worksheets helping them implement the topic. And they want to join a community supporting them on their journey learning and internalizing the topic. Ryan Holiday even sells his Stoicism fans $26 coins and Marcus Aurelius bobbleheads, reminding them of their commitment to Stoicism—which he says on the My First Million podcast are actually bigger and better revenue-generating businesses than selling books. *Wrap your head around that.*

The important nuance here, and we want to be very *ARRRRR*-ing clear about this, is that what people want more of isn't "you." We hear marketers say all the time: "Build a personal brand! Get people to fall in love with YOU! Then, people will buy anything and everything you create!" No, they won't. For example, Billie Eilish is one of the biggest music stars in the world. She has millions and millions of fans and followers. And in 2019 she published a book (called *Billie Eilish*—"People love you!!!") and it was a massive flop. Nobody bought it.

What readers, listeners, viewers, and potential customers want isn't you. **It's your category.** The reason readers keep buying more Ryan Holiday books is because he keeps writing books about Stoicism, and his readers are obsessed with [category] Stoicism. Celebrities, on the other hand, typically write one book. And that book is titled their name. And it never sells. And then they don't write any other books—because people don't want more of "them."

When you successfully build a unique and differentiated category (in which the reader is the Main Character, not you), you can create a dozen different revenue streams giving readers more of what they love [category] in a dozen different ways.

For example:

- Digital Products (books, eBooks, courses, etc.)
- Physical Products (t-shirts, coffee mugs, collectable coins, etc.)
- Services (consulting, advising, coaching, etc.)
- Tools (SaaS platforms, templates, etc.)
- Ongoing Education (paid newsletters, communities, etc.)

The list goes on and on.

In fact, the more differentiated your category, and the more committed you are to giving readers more of what they want in that chosen category, the more likely you are to see the next business model opportunity hiding in plain sight. "Oh, readers found this framework helpful but aren't sure how to implement it? Why don't I turn that into a downloadable worksheet? Or why don't I compile all my frameworks and worksheets together and make that a book? Or why don't I take my book outline and turn that into a 4-week coaching program?"

Making money as a writer, creator, entrepreneur and thought leader is easy when you are known for a niche you own.

Then, you're just in the business of giving people more of what you know they want and need.

"Thinker's High"

The last thing we want to share with you here is this: Climbing The Content Pyramid is not easy. Just like how running 26.2 miles (a marathon) isn't easy. It hurts your legs. It makes you gasp for air. You end up in a puddle of sweat. You stink. And you're exhausted for a few days. But... somewhere along the way, you forgot all about that. You had what most people call "Runner's High." Things were tough, you pushed through, you reached a state of bliss, and on the other side was a waterfall of endorphins. You felt fantastic because you overcame a challenge.

Writing, creating content, and "leading people's thinking in new and different directions" is no different. It's hard. It takes work. If you've ever sat down and tried to read *Crime and Punishment* by Fyodor Dostoevsky, then you know there is nothing enjoyable about reading that novel. It's a workout for your brain. But if you can push through, if you can sit in the discomfort long enough, what's waiting for you on the other side is "Thinker's High": a rush of endorphins for consuming something that changes the way you see the world.

We Pirates hope to do this until we die.

We are addicted to Thinker's High. Every time we experience it, we want it to last longer. And when it goes away, we want to do it again (despite the fact that our heads hurt after it wears off).

As both a creator and a consumer, "Thinker's High" is your measure for success.

If you are creating and consuming things that make your head hurt (a little bit), then you are growing. You are getting stronger. The fibers in your brain are bulging the same way your biceps get a pump in the gym. But if you are creating and consuming things that make your head feel like mush, then you're doing the opposite. You're getting weaker. You're growing lazy. And each day you practice these habits, "Thinker's

High" goes from being an exhausting but highly rewarding activity to the intellectual equivalent of going to the gym for the first time in years, doing 100 burpees, and then throwing up in the bathroom stall.

Which is why we say:

Thinking about thinking is the most important kind of thinking.

CHAPTER TWO

Writer Business Models

How Writers, Creators, And Thought Leaders Monetize

The big question every writer, creator, and thought leader (at some point) asks themselves is, "OK I'm building an audience, I'm making a difference with my work, I'm becoming known for a niche I own—but how do I make money?"

Some writers don't want to think about the money side. They would rather defer responsibility to someone else and not learn about business models and "contaminate" their art. (Society calls these writers & creators "starving artists.") Other writers & creators over-rotate on the business side and spend all their time trying to figure out how to "growth hack" and quickly monetize their work. Both are unfortunate outcomes.

The question of how to make money as a writer, creator, and thought leader is a bit loaded—because it requires you to address a deeper question, first.

2 questions, actually...

The 2 Most Important Money Questions: What Does The Party Cost? And Who Is The Party For?

There are 2 "life" questions you need to ask yourself as you begin down the path to monetization.

- **Question #1:** What does the party cost?
- **Question #2:** And who is the party for?

What Does The Party Cost?

"What does the party cost?" is your "burn rate" (but we think "pay for the party" is a more fun way to think about it). Your "burn rate" is the amount of money it costs to sustain your lifestyle of happy living. For example, what's your rent or mortgage? How much do you spend on groceries each month? How often do you eat out? Do you eat at fancy restaurants and order bottles of Châteauxneuf dula-ding-dong? Or is ordering Chipotle on Friday nights considered "treating yourself?" What's your car payment? How often do you go shopping? What do you spend on a typical afternoon date with your significant other? How much does your dog's health insurance cost? All of these questions (wherever there is money flowing out of your pocket each month) is how much it costs to live your happy lifestyle.

Once you have total clarity around your monthly spending, now consider how much money you have in savings/liquid investments and how many months you would be able to sustain your current style of living if your income was reduced to $0.

That's your burn rate—and what your "party" costs (the party being: living and enjoying life at your current level).

The reason this question is so important is because the cost of your party is going to drastically influence the decisions you make (and feel comfortable making) as you begin to think about monetizing your creations. For example: if your monthly "party" costs $10,000, and you have $5,000 in savings, then choosing to quit your job and go all-in on being a writer or creator (with no income streams in place) basically means you have less than 30 days to "figure it out." Whereas if your monthly party costs $10,000 but you have $120,000 in savings and liquid investments, then you have an entire year to try things, fall on your face, pick yourself back up again, and keep going without ever needing to adjust your style of living (and not needing to worry about paying rent is crucial to keeping your head clear, your mind sharp, and your goals firmly in focus).

Who Is The Party For?

"Who is the party for?" is a deeper, more complicated question—and usually the root issue that keeps so many people from pursuing their passions.

If your "party costs" are high, why are they high? Do you feel like you need to "keep up with the Joneses?" Is your identity and self-worth wrapped up in your nice house and fancy car? Maybe you want to go all-in on being a writer, but are afraid of downsizing and reducing your "party costs." If so, what's the fear? That your parents won't be proud of you anymore? That your friends will call you crazy for giving up your cushy corporate job? That you'll feel like a failure before you've even started?

A quick personal pirate story:
Pirate Eddie is a child of blue-collar immigrants from Korea. His mom was a scheduling clerk at a hospital. His dad was a prosecutor in Korea but ended up driving a taxi then buying a limo to become a solopreneur. When Pirate Eddie graduated from college and got his first consulting job, he made $42,000 per year—which was more than what his parents had ever made in a single year *combined*. He and his parents were excited and amazed that the "American Dream" was coming true.

Yet, when his parents came to visit him in Chicago, his mom started to cry after seeing his post-college apartment. It was spartan with two mismatched chairs, a beaten-up recliner stuck in recline (after being bought and sold too many times in college), with a TV and a mattress on the floor. Pirate Eddie's mom's perception of what her son's "party" would be was 180 degrees different from what she had expected—or what Pirate Eddie wanted or needed. In his mind, why throw a big and expensive party in a place you weren't in half the time because of the travel required to live a consultant's life? (Had Pirate Eddie made different choices, he might have made his mother much happier, sooner—but compromised his long-term financial freedom and happiness as a result.)

The reality is, most people make financial decisions based on what they want other people to think about them—opposed to what they truly want for themselves. And so we emphasize the importance of this question, FIRST, because in order to effectively monetize your writing and other creations, you may need to make decisions that look foolish in the short-term but set you up for massive success in the long run. And these decisions are nearly impossible to make if you have your parents, siblings, neighbors, or coworkers sitting on both shoulders, whispering into your ears, "That's a stupid decision. We love your house! It's so nice. You have such a great job! Not everyone has a job they enjoy, you know. You don't want to risk that, do you? What will everyone think?"

The Ultimate Goal

Your "ultimate goal" is not to make money as a writer or creator. It's also not to make "a lot" of money as a writer or creator.

Your ultimate goal is to *make a difference, first,* and then to monetize the different you make in such a way that you build a portfolio of intellectual capital that "pays for the party" **without you doing anything.** (This is sometimes called "horizontal income" because it rolls into your bank account even when you're laying down.) These creations (assets) could be directly related to your craft: books and courses, eBooks and paid newsletters, etc. Or these assets could be indirectly related and purchased from the earnings generated from your craft: stocks and bonds, real estate, cryptocurrencies, and so on. The point is: what you want is to create and/or acquire assets that pay you dividends *regardless of whether or not you show up to the office.*

This is what breaks the cycle of selling your time for money.

For example, in 2020, Pirate Cole self-published a book called *The Art & Business of Online Writing.* That "asset" pays Pirate Cole approximately $2,500 per month, every month, as long as he continues to write online and the "digital writing" category remains relevant. Now imagine having 10 of those in your portfolio. Or 100 of them. Your party would be paid for, forever!

Unfortunately, most writers and creators (or frankly most people) do not think about the game of "building wealth" this way. Ask any writer or creator what their financial goal is, and most will either admit to not having one or simply say, "To make a lot of money." The problem with a vague goal like this is it does not take into account your burn rate: how much does your party cost? If you make $1 million but spend $1 million on "your party," you are "making a lot of money" and still poor. But if you make $1 million but only spend $100,000 and use the other $900,000 to build, buy, or invest in assets that will pay you forever, you've just gained 9+ years of runway.

Which unlocks more time.

Which unlocks more creative freedom.

Which is what allows you to build more assets in your portfolio of intellectual capital (which is the most valuable asset of all).

And on and on your flywheel spins.

How To Leap

Once you've come to terms with the above 2 questions (How much does the party cost? And who is the party for?), there are 3 different ways to "take the leap" as a writer and creator.

1. **The first is to save up a bunch of money** (enough to "pay for your party" for 6-12 months), push all your chips into the center of the table, quit your full-time job, and hope that you "figure it out" before the money runs out. Some people thrive off this sense of urgency, and believe they will take more productive action if they feel like their "feet are to the fire." However, it's worth remembering that when the money isn't coming in, every time you pay your rent, fill your car up with gas, or go out to dinner, you're going to feel like the floor is falling out from under you. (This is a feeling we know well and it doesn't get better with time!)

2. **The second is to get fired.** This is a "forced leap" situation. But as Pirate Christopher likes to say, "For many, entrepreneurship isn't just a way up. It's a way *out*." Sometimes, getting fired can be a blessing in disguise. It's one of those moments where you are forced to make a decision: do you spend the next few months dusting off your resumé trying to replace what you had before? Or do you push forward and risk it all for the biscuit? We know many people who got fired at the start of the COVID-19 pandemic in 2020

and decided to become digital writers & creators, start writing on Twitter, launch a newsletter, or start some other kind of digital business—and ended up unlocking a career transformation as a result.

3. **The third is to build momentum while still working full-time,** and then "take the leap" once your side-hustle income begins to replace your 9-5 salary. This is what Pirate Cole did back in 2016, as he was preparing to leave his job and go all-in on being a writer & ghostwriter. Once his after-hours writing revenue was approximately 50% of his monthly salary, he felt confident quitting his job knowing that with 8 more hours in the day, he'd find a way to cover the other 50%. (As the story goes, not only did he replace his full-time salary shortly after quitting, but ended up tripling his monthly earnings as a writer before going on to build a 7-figure ghostwriting agency.)

Depending on which of the 3 leap paths you take, you can see how important it is to have clarity around your burn rate (What Does The Party Cost?) as well as the underlying reasons why your lifestyle is the way it is (Who Is The Party For?). Because the answers to these questions are going to dramatically change how you leap, when you leap, and/ or if you ever have the confidence to take the leap at all.

Writer Business Goals: What Outcome Are You Solving For?

The next big question you need to ask yourself is what outcome you are solving for in monetizing your writing:

- Are you solving for money?

- Are you solving for time?
- Are you solving for status?
- Are you solving for contribution/impact?

Here's a quick breakdown:

[**Money**] Some writers, creators, and thought leaders use writing to create new revenue streams in their life. They write a book and that book generates income in the form of royalties, or they create a paid newsletter so they can make money from home whilst lounging in their sweatpants (like we did!). The point is, these writers have a financial goal above all things, and make decisions accordingly.

[**Time**] Some writers and creators use writing to solve for time. They are consultants or entrepreneurs or marketers who answer the same questions over and over again, and come to the conclusion that if they shared their insights at scale (via writing online, publishing a book, etc.), they wouldn't need to manually repeat their same frameworks, case studies, and mental models. They could just send people links to their books, blog posts, articles, Twitter Threads, or LinkedIn posts, and their library of content could "talk for them."

[**Status**] Some writers, creators, and thought leaders use writing to solve for status. They don't want to write a book because they have something meaningful to share. They want to write a book because a book gives them the status of "being an author," which allows them to charge more per speaking gig or consulting opportunity due to "perceived credibility." (The vast majority of consultants who publish books fall into this category, and use money to outsource this task to a ghostwriter because they don't want to spend the time to do it themselves! Writing is purely a lever to acquire more status.)

[**Contribution**] And some writers, creators, and thought leaders use writing to make a contribution to society. They want to write a book because they have something meaningful to share, a difference they want to make, and because writing allows them to contribute at scale. Their motivations are more intrinsic than extrinsic. Whether they "make money" or "save time" or "become famous" from their work is less of a priority.

Whichever outcome (or combination of outcomes) you want to unlock for yourself is up to you.

However, it's crucial that you be honest with yourself about what you desire and why—because the outcome is going to drastically influence your choice of business models.

For example, there's a reason why so many writers accept book deals from major publishers, even though these deals are terrible economically for the writer/creator. These writers don't actually want to solve for money. They want to solve for status. They care more about being "chosen," having the stamp of approval from a major publishing house, and being able to tell their mom, dad, friends, and former high school teachers, "See? I became a published writer after all!" And, to be clear, it's 100% OK to want this outcome. Just don't be confused when your first royalty check comes in six months later and you receive $13.47. Book deals are great for status, terrible for money. (We've lived this. We've sold lots of books for publishers and received lots of teeny-weeny royalty checks for it. Please take heed, fellow Pirates.)

How you make your money as a writer & creator is *exceedingly* dependent on what your business goals are, what outcomes you are solving for, and most importantly, what type of content you create.

Obvious vs Non-Obvious Outcomes

In the last chapter, we explained The Content Pyramid, and how writers, creators, and thought leaders move up The Content Pyramid by creating either Obvious or Non-Obvious content.

Well, Obvious and Non-Obvious content also plays a major role in what sorts of financial outcomes you can expect from your writing.

Here are the differences:

Obvious Content

- **[Money]** If you are an Obvious creator making Obvious Connections in your content, then you are more likely to make money in the short-term. Obvious content is incremental ("How to move from A to B"), immediate, urgent, and can usually be rationalized by a reader as an immediate "investment" in themselves. For example, it's much easier *(in the short term)* to sell a $19 eBook on "How To Make Your Facebook Ads 10x More Profitable" than it is to sell a $19 book full of Non-Obvious insights readers won't necessarily "get" (or be able to apply) right away.

- **[Status]** Obvious content is also much more likely to receive immediate attention on social media. Why? Because the average person doesn't want to "think" when they're scrolling. They want to see things that validate their current beliefs and "Like" them—not things that make them pause and question their entire point of view of the world. (On social media people are scrolling to become Confappy: a portmanteau of "confirmation" and "happy.") As a result, simple and Obvious content has an exponentially higher chance of receiving engagement and going viral—again, *in the short term.* *Warning:* one of two things needs to be true for this to work. Either you are a master languager who can take Obvious content and make it seem magically different, OR you already have status and fans who fawn over your content.

- **[Time]** Obvious content does not compound in value over time. That best-selling eBook, "How To Make Your Facebook Ads 10x More Profitable," is here today, gone later today. What makes Obvious content urgent and important in the short term is the same thing that makes it shelf unstable in the long term. Obvious content is timely, not timeless. And Obvious content creators are always riding the wave of the "next big thing." For example, when "Web3" gets popular, they rush to publish "The Executive's Guide To Web3" before anyone else. They are capitalizing on a moment. The problem is, you're trading your time *right now* for money or status *right now*. And while you can manufacture more money and status, you can't manufacture more time. (And someone after you is going to write "The Executive's Guide To Web4!")

- [Contribution/Impact] The contribution from Obvious content functions more like a great cup of coffee, jolting you right away and energizing you to take action. This can be incredibly valuable to someone who needs a quick burst or is feeling stuck in the mud. However, it doesn't last—nor does it leave a lasting impression. It's a bit like attending a Tony Robbins conference: while the music is blaring and your hands are in the air, you feel terrific. You feel like you're experiencing a giant breakthrough in your life. And that feeling might last a few days, maybe a week. But eventually, it wears off, and you're right back to being unhappy, frustrated, and "stuck" (which most people think means, "I need another Tony Robbins conference!"). Obvious content that makes a contribution "easily" in the short term usually doesn't lead to a lasting contribution in the long term.

So, if you want Money, Status, and Contribution/Impact in the short term, create Obvious content. However, do realize that in order to maintain your income streams and "position" of authority, you will need to stay on the hamster wheel and keep creating Obvious content long into the future. You will sacrifice Time and long-term compounding. (And remember: the moment you stop, your Money, Status, and Impact will fall off a cliff.)

But if your time is precious or you have the luxury of taking the long view, then you'll want to focus on Non-Obvious Content.

Non-Obvious Content

- [**Money**] Non-Obvious creators usually don't become best-sellers overnight. They are way less viral. In fact, some of the best Non-Obvious creators became famous after their death. That's because when you present the world with a radically new & different POV, you have to accept that you might not reap the dividends of your efforts for many years—maybe ever. (If you're planning to give the world a push in a new and different direction, don't be surprised when it pushes back.) A perfect example of this is the "money" difference between these two books: *The Subtle Art of Not Giving A F*ck* and *Thinking, Fast and Slow*. The former (Obvious content) has sold over 10 million copies in just a few years, but will likely become irrelevant this decade. And the latter has sold a fraction of the amount (under 3 million copies) in double the length of time (published 2012), but will likely remain relevant well beyond any of our lifetimes. If you want to make money NOW, write an Obvious book like *The Subtle Art of Not Giving A F*ck* (the book's big idea is: if you want to be happy, just don't give a fuck). But if you don't want to optimize for (near-term) money, and would rather optimize for Time, Impact, Legacy, and/or Contribution to society, write a Non-Obvious book like *Thinking, Fast and Slow* (which articulates in great detail the two modes of thinking human beings juggle as we make our way through life).

- [Status] The status component that comes from creating Non-Obvious content is earned. It can't be bought or leveraged from someone else. We respect Non-Obvious thinkers not because of what they've achieved or how many copies of their book they've sold (or how many followers they have on social media), but because of the way they changed our thinking. In some cases, these Non-Obvious creators transition into the mainstream and their Non-Obvious insights become Obvious, commonly accepted, and celebrated in the mainstream—as Viktor E. Frankl did with his book, *Man's Search For Meaning*, but it's rare. Non-Obvious creators and thinkers hardly ever reach the same levels of status as Obvious creators.

- [Time] Like a fine wine, Non-Obvious creators benefit the most from time. Their work becomes more and more true, more and more relevant, and over a long enough horizon, becomes representative of an entire decade or even generation of humanity. We will be reading *Think and Grow Rich*, or *How To Win Friends & Influence People* for lifetimes. Why? Because when these books were written, they presented almost zero Obvious, timely, actionable advice—and instead presented Non-Obvious, timeless ways of "thinking." When you write and share Non-Obvious insights, you "lose" to other Obvious creators in the short term, but exponentially surpass them in the long term (so don't be surprised when they're the ones topping the charts and receiving all the applause, *today*).

- [Contribution] Non-Obvious, contribution-oriented creators (Missionaries) tend to create more net-new

Non-Obvious contribution-oriented creators—in the
same way legendary leaders create more leaders, not
followers. Their work can become commercially successful over time, but the real harbinger of their work is the
number of net-new Non-Obvious thinkers they inspire.
For example: Rolling Stone reported, "The Ramones
likely inspired more bands than anybody since the Beat-
les; the Sex Pistols, the Clash, Nirvana, Metallica, the
Misfits, Green Day and countless others have owed much
of their sound and creed to what the band made possible."
These types of creators focus myopically on creating a
different future—not just for themselves, but for others as
well. And while we don't know what was in W. Edwards
Deming's (the godfather of the Quality Movement) heart
of hearts, we're pretty sure he wanted to make a difference
above all else. The value created by Deming's students
dwarfs the money he made. And that's the point. Deming
died in 1993, but every time you turn on a device of any
kind, and it works, you can thank Dr. Deming for teaching the world how to create high-quality products.

Non-Obvious, contribution-oriented creators tend to take a long-
term view of their work, and aim to create a compounding library of
timeless content that will grow in value as the direct result of other
people sharing and contributing to the new Non-Obvious thinking
they set into motion.

The Money/Status/Time/Contribution Dilemma

Here's the dilemma:

The vast majority of writers, creators, and thought leaders say they
want to "stand the test of time" or "have a legendary impact," but then
2 seconds later point to some Obvious creator going viral on social

media making a bunch of money (in the short term) and say, "But I also want that."

So, here are some if/then scenarios...

- If you want short-term money, then create Obvious content.
- If you want long-term dividends, then create Non-Obvious content (your library will last longer).
- If you want short-term status, then create Obvious content.
- If you want long-term status, then create Non-Obvious content (you'll become known as a legendary "thinker").
- If you want your contribution/impact to be known immediately, then create Obvious content.
- If you want your contribution/impact to live on well beyond your lifetime, and to spark new creations as the result of your net-new thinking, then create Non-Obvious content (if everything you write is timeless, then every new addition to your library—*by you, or by other new creators building on your work*—has compounding benefits).

Some writers genuinely like creating Obvious content more than Non-Obvious content (and vice versa), and that's OK. Both matter in the world, and both are important for different reasons. However, from a business model and monetization perspective, it's worth being honest with yourself about which outcomes you want most and why— and all of this ties back to How Much Does The Party Cost and Who Is The Party For?

For example: it's hard to solve your burn rate in the short term by creating Non-Obvious content.

Because Non-Obvious content rarely makes (much) money in the short term, and all of the upside tends to come 5-10 years later (if your

Non-Obvious content is successful at introducing new thinking and moving the world).

Which is why your efforts and desired outcomes need to be aligned.

The Content Pyramid: How To Design Your Business Model As A Writer At Each Of The 5 Levels

The 5 levels of the Content Pyramid are:
- **Level 1:** Consumption
- **Level 2:** Curation
- **Level 3:** Obvious Connection
- **Level 4:** Non-Obvious Connection
- **Level 5:** Category Creation

But how you make your money at each level changes—with new and different (and freedom-filled) business models being unlocked at each new level.

Again, to recap: it's important to first understand your individual burn rate and what type of content you are passionate about creating (Obvious or Non-Obvious) before working toward monetizing your craft. Then, it becomes a question of climbing up The Content Pyramid, unlocking new & different ways of making money for yourself as a writer and creator.

McDonald's or Michelin Star

The first framework we want to share with you is what we like to call **McDonald's or Michelin Star.**

When you "create" something—whether it be a blog post, a Twitter Thread, an article, a book, a paid newsletter, an Ultimate Guide, a course, or anything in-between—it's important to understand what the "trade" is you're offering the reader and customer. And the trade goes like this: if a reader is going to give you their attention and/or money, what they're really giving you is *time off their life*. **Let the gravity of that request sink in.** When you ask someone to read or buy your work, you aren't just asking for "2 minutes" or "$20." What you're really asking for is *a chunk of their life*. Because they'll never get those 2 minutes, or 20 minutes, or 2 hours, or 20 hours back again. Ever.

So, in order for the reader to understand whether or not this "trade" is worth their time (which is more valuable than money), it's crucial for them to know what they're going to get in return.

What is the "value" of your content? What's the "give-to-get?" What is the consumer giving (time, or time & money), and what do they expect to get in return?

The answer is almost always one of two extremes: either you are offering them something Obvious, cheap, easy-to-understand and consume (McDonald's), or you're offering them something Non-Obvious, expensive, and difficult-to-understand and consume that leaves them "wanting more" (a Michelin Star restaurant). Both serve their purpose (McDonald's feeds 68 million people per day, or roughly 1% of the world's population, whereas Michelin Star restaurants serve 99x fewer customers and are exponentially less profitable, but offer a completely different and more memorable experience).

When thinking through how you make your money as a writer & creator, you must be honest with yourself about which one you are:

Are you McDonald's? Or a Michelin Star restaurant?

As a creator, it's worth realizing you can do both. You can create some products that are mass-market McDonald's, and other products that are niche Michelin Stars.

A-list actors do this all the time. For example, Matthew McConaughey once turned down $14.5 million to star in a romantic comedy film because he decided he didn't want to optimize for money anymore—he wanted to optimize for impact and contribution to his craft.

In an interview, he told the story:

> *"I look up and notice: I'm rom-com romantic comedy guy. And I'm owning this, because you're damn right those rom-coms are paying for the house that I'm renting on the beach that I'm going shirtless on. Guilty of that, you know? But I did notice, well, I want to do some other things. No, no, no. You can't do that. And I noticed: the industry and the public are nothing other than rom-com shirtless guy on the beach. That's where I went OK. **Well if I can't do what I want to do, I gotta quit doing what I've been doing.** And I went off back down to Texas, and hid out, and called my agent and money people and everything and said, "I'm not doing those anymore. 20 months, nothing. No work. Nada. 20 months. I called it early on. Dropped tears to make the decision. I even thought about having to change careers. Now, at that time, this is when Hollywood really got the message. About six months into that sabbatical, I'm saying I'm not doing those, an offer comes in for a script at $8 million. I said no thank you. They come back with $10 million. I say no thank you. They come back at $12.5 million. Small pause. They come back at $14.5 million. I said no."*

Today, Matthew McConaughey is known as one of the greatest and most diverse actors alive.

But he had to pay a price (and that price was $14.5 million and almost 2 years of no work) in order to move from being an Obvious rom-com sex symbol to the Non-Obvious actor who won an Oscar for Best Lead Actor in the film *Dallas Buyers Club* (2014)—which originally premiered at Toronto International Film Festival before crossing into the mainstream and capturing the hearts and minds of the entire film industry. The film had a modest budget of $5 million (a far cry from McConaughey's prior big budget rom-coms) but ended up grossing over $52 million worldwide, and won a laundry list of awards.

The big mistake is trying to both—or something in the middle.

If you ever find yourself rationalizing the "value" of the thing you've created, convincing yourself that it's "for everyone," that's a neon sign you're using ill-constructed mental scaffolding. (Goofy, sexy rom-com Matthew McConaughey works in a goofy, sexy rom-com. But that shtick doesn't work in a very serious drama.) Customers don't want something "for everyone." They want the thing they want, and they want to know it's specifically for them.

Which means it's in your best interest to be clear—*in yourself, and to your readers/customers*—which one you are, and why.

Now, let's apply this thinking up the 5 levels of The Creator Pyramid.

Level 1: Monetizing As A Consumer

Making money as a consumer (Level 1) doesn't exist.

(If you think you're going to make money from home scrolling watching TikToks, sorry.)

Monetization only begins when you create value for others. However, there is a meaningful difference between Passive Consumption and Active Consumption, in the sense that Active Consumption is an investment in your future self. While you may not make any money actively consuming YouTube videos, reading Medium articles, or bookmarking Twitter Threads on a given subject or industry, you may be able to monetize that knowledge sometime in the future. You are learning, practicing, and consuming other people's work to one day monetize in Obvious or Non-Obvious ways. All of this Active Consumption work has the *potential* to give you new data points to draw connections and create ideas that are valuable to the world.

The problem is that Active Consumption can easily become a procrastination technique to avoid Creation.

Most writers spend their entire lives thinking the key to becoming a legendary writer is to read. And yes, while there is tremendous benefit to "studying the greats" and exposing yourself to a wide variety of perspectives and writing styles, the brutal truth is that most aspiring writers who read "a lot" end up mastering the craft of reading and never write a single thing. They fall in love with Active Consumption and become quite good at it—but fail to work their way up The Content Pyramid.

This is also why Humanities professors at elite higher education institutions leave their graduates with few outcomes aside from a mountain of debt and bookcases of books. We believe history majors should read about World War 1 and World War 2, but then spend an equal amount of time Practicing In Public (as Pirate Cole teaches), putting forth their predictions (out in the open—not privately in a closed classroom) about how and when, for example, Russia's invasion of Ukraine will end. Similarly, English majors should read *Finnegans Wake*, and also be required to publish their own work of fiction before they graduate. Philosophy majors should study Kant, but then come up with their own version of what they believe are Categorical Imperatives in a Native Digital society.

If the education world wants to produce more creators in society, it needs to fix their ratio of reading versus writing—input vs output—and move generations of consumers up The Content Pyramid.

You can only monetize as a consumer when you move from Consumer to Creator.

Think of the knowledge you acquire through Active Consumption as potential energy.

It has more future value than present value.

In order to turn that knowledge into kinetic energy, you must make the transition from Consumer to Creator. And for many Active Consumers, especially those who become so comfortable consuming that their identity begins to form around their "skill" of Active Consumption, this can feel quite daunting. (It's much easier to be an armchair critic. Writing about boxing is very different from boxing.)

Which is why an easier stepping stone is to be a Curator, first.

Level 2: How To Monetize
As A Curator

The primary value a Curator provides is saving time.

They're McDonald's. (Although, in rare exceptions, some Curators deserve a Michelin Star.)

As a consumer, the reason you pay Curators with your attention and/

or money is to save you the time and trouble of doing the hard work yourself. The Curator's job is to aggregate content on a given subject *so that you don't have to*. For example: the reason you subscribe to a newsletter like Robinhood Snacks is because you want the most important financial news aggregated for you each morning. That's the "trade." You give them your email address and short-term attention, and they do the hard work of curating the most important & relevant financial news so that you don't have to.

A Curator is not a Creator in the sense that you (as the reader/consumer) are not "trading" your attention/money in exchange for that creator's individual perspectives, opinions, frameworks, or insights. What you're trading is your attention in exchange for their **organization and judgment**. Instead of having to sift through hundreds or even thousands of articles, podcast episodes, YouTube videos, etc., on a given subject, you are "paying" someone else to do that hard work for you.

As a consumer, things you may want curated are:

- The most important "current events" of the day (like CNN's "5 Things" morning newsletter).
- Timely business ideas based on trends and data (like The Hustle's Trends newsletter).
- Trendy, funny lists on a given subject (like this Buzzfeed article: "20 Texts Sent To The Wrong People That Took Hilarious (or Creepy) Turns").
- The best tools or products in a given industry (like "The 10 Best Home Safes").
- The most-popular content on a given topic (like "The 10 most popular Tedx talks").

Notice, the value here is relevant information *on a specific topic*, aggregated and organized for your benefit.

How Curators become Creators, and how they move up The Content

Pyramid, is by adding more and more of their expertise, insights, perspectives, stories, and beliefs into the things they curate. Credibility is the key here. For example, when a solopreneur like Justin Welsh curates his 14 favorite no-code tools into a Twitter Thread list, the value of that list isn't just that 14 no-code tools are grouped together. It's that these 14 no-code tools are how Justin operates his 1-man business that generates over $1 million in revenue per year—without writing a single line of code. It's his experience as a creator that makes *his* list of 14 no-code tools "valuable" to you.

The easiest place to start as a Curator is by curating what you are a Superconsumer of—and sharing that.

As a Superconsumer of a given subject or industry, you inherently understand what is worth "paying attention to" more than the average person.

This is what gives you authority, which means you are sitting on monetizable value.

- **Are you a Super of food?** Curate the best restaurants in your neighborhood. Curate the best restaurants by food style. Curate the best restaurants by price, or by interior design, or by wine pairing, or by how "Instagrammable" their walls are.
- **Are you a Super of video games?** Curate the best games that are going to come out this year. Curate the best games that existed this past decade. Curate the best games that have existed since the days of Sega Genesis or Atari. Curate the funniest livestream clips of gamers rage-quitting after losing a match.
- **Are you a Super of makeup?** Curate the best makeup kits by occasion. Curate the best makeup by price point (where can people find the best bang for their buck?).

Curate the best YouTube channels where you can learn how to do cool makeup designs on your own, at home.

- **Are you a Super of business books?** Curate books people should read based on specialty. Curate books people can read in different time frames (quick reads vs beach reads vs year-long reads). Curate books by "price per page," and share which ones are worth the time. Curate books by impact on the business world.

As a Superconsumer of *anything*, you are sitting on untapped "potential" intellectual capital that has the power to become kinetic just by organizing and distributing it—moving you one step closer to becoming a Creator. For example: Tim Ferriss was a Superconsumer of personal development content, obsessed with learning about how to "master" himself physically, mentally, and emotionally. So he turned the thing he was "Super passionate" about into a podcast—interviewing hundreds of high-performers and curating their best insights. His book, *Tools of Titans*, is one giant curation of "the tactics, routines, and habits of billionaires, icons, and world-class performers." These are not Tim's personal insights, but rather the most valuable insights shared from his guests. (Curation is what made Mr. Ferriss worth hundreds of millions of dollars.)

However, curation in-and-of-itself is not what's valuable.

What makes curation valuable is *the urgency, specificity, and importance* of what is being curated.

Most Curators do not make as much money as Creators because "organized" existing content isn't as valuable as net-new Obvious or Non-Obvious content.

However, that's not to say you cannot make money as a Curator.

Business Model: Attention and Advertising

Most curated content is free.

When you subscribe to a newsletter like Morning Brew, the "trade" is that in exchange for your email address and attention, they will give you a daily email that summarizes the news (and "makes you smarter"). The way Morning Brew makes money is then by selling your attention to advertisers who sponsor their newsletter.

The reason this model is so popular for Curators is because most curated content, as we said above, is not as valuable as net-new Obvious or Non-Obvious content. You don't have to spend any money to consume it, and you also don't have to spend very much time & attention digesting it (which is both the pro and the con). It's McDonald's. As a result, it's very easy to "get" your attention. But the easier it is to "get" your attention, the less valuable your attention actually is. Which is why you aren't the company's customer. The advertiser is the customer, and the product they're buying is you and your attention.

YouTube unboxing channels, Instagram meme accounts, Twitter profiles that curate tools and books and podcast episodes, and review bloggers almost always end up monetizing attention via advertising—either they run ads themselves, or they charge brands to post on their behalf and gain "access" to their audience. This is the most common "starter" business model for Curators, primarily because it's the most recognizable (we all know what a sponsored post looks like at this point) and easiest to understand when you're first starting out.

Build an audience. Sell your audience.

The problem is, it's hard for Curators to unlock new business models for themselves (such as charging for *their* unique insights) because their entire value (the "trade") is based on their ability to organize content—not their expertise, perspectives, stories, original frameworks, and so on. The benefit you deliver is convenience, not wisdom. And winning on convenience is like winning on cost: *there can only be one.* Consumers only care about who is "the cheapest." Whereas wisdom is not as zero-sum. There can be multiple winners in the wisdom business. (Just look at your bookshelf.)

So as long as you are predominantly a Curator, you won't be able to monetize like a Creator.

Level 3: How To Monetize As An Obvious Creator

Now, it's worth noting that Curation is an exceedingly powerful way to build an initial audience—and to continue building an audience as time goes on.

And the reason is because curating other more well-known people's insights is always going to have more reach potential than sharing your own (at least for the first 10 years of your career). In fact, we'd argue that even once you achieve "Category King status" in your field, it's worth continuing to leverage curation to "Dam The Demand" for other creators and introduce net-new readers/customers to your work. For example, Pirate Cole is the Category King of "Digital Writing," and as a Creator shares his own Digital Writing frameworks, strategies, stories, insights, and perspectives. But he continues to curate other legendary writers' work (like Malcolm Gladwell or Ryan Holiday) to capture the attention of readers & writers who, if they're interested in *those* writers, may also be interested in Pirate Cole.

However, what makes Curation such an effective reach and audience-building strategy is also what makes it such a poor monetization strategy. Conventional wisdom in the digital, social world says to "build an audience, first" and then decide what you want to do with it later. The problem is, not all audiences are created equal. (Pirate Christopher's two podcasts, while in the top 1%, are still dwarfed by the top 0.1% podcasts. The difference is, his audience is not a bunch of dudes who still live with their parents. His listeners are some of the most powerful entrepreneurs, executives, and VCs in the world. It's a smaller, but exponentially more valuable audience.)

How you build your audience and *who's in it* determines how you ultimately monetize that audience.

When you exclusively use curation to build an audience, only one business model is at your disposal: monetizing "attention." And as we explained in the above section (Level 2), the easier it is to "get" someone's attention, the less valuable that attention is—and here's a concrete example. According to NerdWallet, "Influencers with a million followers can earn somewhere around $670 per post. A content creator on Instagram with 100,000 followers can earn about $200 per post, while someone with 10,000 followers can make about $88 per post."

If you aim to build an audience of 1 million followers using curation as a strategy, you will probably reach your goal of 1 million followers before most Obvious and Non-Obvious creators. The problem is, since the audience you've built is not niche, specialized, or highly differentiated in any way, the only viable way for you to make money is to monetize the "attention" with advertising and sponsored posts. And $670 per branded post might seem like a lot of money until you realize you can only promote 2-3 brands per month without giving off the impression that you're shilling products in exchange for cash, which comes out to a grand total of $2,010 per month—or about $24,000 per year.

That's less than minimum wage.

Monetizing attention is a race to the bottom—and of all the potential business models, it's one of the worst ones out there. (There is always someone willing to be more outrageous than you, fighting tooth-and-nail to grab people's attention. If you jump the Grand Canyon on your motorcycle this week, next week someone will skydive from the Empire State building.)

Meanwhile, Obvious and Non-Obvious Creators with much smaller audiences, but who provide value directly to their audience, can earn significantly more money by not monetizing the attention and instead monetizing the quality of the "trade." Said differently: when consumers believe the value of their "get" (value received) is materially greater than their "give" (engagement & money), you know you're onto something special. *Man's Search for Meaning* costs $12 on Amazon and is 192 pages of timeless wisdom. That is one of the most legendary give-to-gets in Non-Obvious history.

Business Model: Direct-To-Creator for Products and Services

The transition from Curator to Creator happens when you spend more time sharing your own expertise than you do other people's.

Which is also what unlocks a more powerful and profitable business model.

Your audience pays you directly.

Selling your time as a product or service is the primary business model for an Obvious Creator. This means instead of monetizing the "attention" of your collective audience, you are monetizing *access*—their relationship with you, and the value you provide them directly. (The fact that this type of attention is harder to earn is what makes it more valuable.) OnlyFans. Patreon. Substack. Gumroad. Mighty Networks. Private Slack & Discord channels. These are all just different examples of the same thing: the creator is charging for access to their niche, specialized, unique, differentiated content—and being paid by the reader/viewer/consumer in exchange. That's the "give-to-get." Whether 1 million people or 1,000 people follow you or know who you are on social media is irrelevant. All that matters is how many people are paying you directly. Our friend, the legendary Joe Pine (author of landmark book, *The Experience Economy*) says you know you have a valuable experience when people pay for it. For example the Bunkitsu Bookstore in Japan *charges people just to visit.*

(Most of the time, small, niche creators with Direct-To-Creator business models make significantly more than curators with massive, undifferentiated audiences trying to monetize the sum total of their "attention." Because monetizing Direct-To-Creator cuts out the middleman so you capture more of the margin, requiring you to sell less volume.)

Most importantly, leveraging a Direct-To-Creator business model is what elevates you out of "transactional business models." Advertising and attention, curation and convenience are all inherently transactional. Your customers don't have a direct relationship with you. However, going Direct-To-Creator is relational. There is way more intimacy in the business model. And you control your own destiny because there are no intermediaries. You can build a business based on customer lifetime value while simultaneously giving you an incredible amount of data about who your Superconsumers are and what they value most—allowing you to continue monetizing long into the future.

The Big Fork In The Road: Obvious vs Non-Obvious

You know you want to be a Creator.

And you know you want your business model to be Direct-To-Creator—straight from the customer's pocket into your pocket.

No ads. No sponsored posts. No chasing viral hits and clicks.

Just value exchanged for money.

The big question you need to ask yourself is whether you want to be an Obvious creator or a Non-Obvious creator. Again, most people "think" they want to be a Non-Obvious creator, but when push comes to shove what they really want is to be a short-term famous, instant gratification Obvious creator who is "known" for being a timeless Non-Obvious creator. They want their cake and to eat it too. (Pirate Christopher held a poll on Twitter and asked people which they preferred: Obvious content or Non-Obvious content. 90% of people responded "Non-Obvious

Content," which is a shocking majority. The problem is, we all know that's not true: our actions, and the things we typically click on and give our attention to online is really the opposite: 90% Obvious, 10% Non-Obvious.)

So, here's a different way of thinking about it:

Which game do you want to play?

- The "actionable" game?
- Or the "thinking" game?

Obvious content is Actionable. The clearest tell is when the content says "How To" do something. Most "How To" is Obvious, incremental, and linear: "Want to achieve X? Here's how to move from A to B."

Non-Obvious content is Thinking. It's the reason "Why" something works, happens, functions, etc. "Why" content is Non-Obvious and meandering because understanding requires context and the connection of disparate and oftentimes conflicting or polar opposite data points. As a result, Non-Obvious content is more complicated than Obvious content, but also more timeless and exponential.

These are the functional differences between Obvious and Non-Obvious content.

But there are emotional differences as well.

Obvious creators don't have to risk being wrong (or being "exponentially wrong"), because Obvious content speaks to Obvious, commonly understood, and already desirable answers and outcomes. For example: "How To Write A Book." The writer already knows the audience wants to write a book, and their job is to move them incrementally forward (from A to B) in order to unlock that already desirable outcome.

Non-Obvious creators, on the other hand, have to have the guts to stand in the middle of the town square with egg on their face. When you are a Non-Obvious creator, your content is working to provide answers that are not already commonly understood, (and in some cases: first educate people about problems that are not already commonly understood, before giving them answers to those problems that are not already commonly understood). You are Pythagoras in 500 BC trying to make the case for why the earth is round, not flat. At that time, that "answer" was not commonly understood, nor was it considered desirable to hold as a belief—which meant a lot of people thought Pythagoras was a moron for a very long time (until one day, he was hailed as a genius). "There is such a fine line between stupid and clever."

Again, most people want to believe they have what it takes to be a Non-Obvious Creator, and maybe functionally they do. But it's the emotional side, the fear of being publicly rebuked, questioned, criticized, or simply wrong (and shamed as a result) that holds them back.

Which is why it's much easier to continue your journey as a Creator by first starting with Obvious content.

How To Monetize As An Obvious Creator

Obvious creators make money helping readers/customers make Obvious connections that unlock Obvious and already desirable outcomes.

- "How To Increase The Effectiveness Of Your Facebook Ads By 10x In 90 Days"
- "How To Experience Less Conflict In Your Marriage"
- "How To Save Your First $10,000 As A College Graduate"
- "How To Build A Small Portfolio Of Rental Properties"

And so on.

This content is the easiest to monetize because the reader/customer already knows what they want—and as long as you speak to what the reader/customer already knows they want, and can prove competence and credibility, it's fairly likely they will buy what you're selling. It's kind of like going to a concert of your favorite band. You want them to play the hits so you can sing along. (What you don't want is for them to play songs you've never heard before—and can't sing along to.)

There are a number of vehicles through which you can distribute and monetize Obvious content:

- Books
- Courses
- Speaking gigs
- Digital products
- Paid newsletter
- Physical products
- Mastermind groups
- Bootcamps and workshops

Now, the takeaway here isn't, "Which should I do? Write a book? Or create a course?"

The more important question is: "What am I creating? Obvious content? Or Non-Obvious content?" And then the vehicle through which you communicate that Obvious or Non-Obvious content is up to you.

For example, even though Obvious and Non-Obvious creators both have these same monetization vehicles at their disposal does not mean they are equal. For example: *1001 One-Liners and Short Jokes: The Ultimate Collection of the Funniest, Laugh-Out-Loud Rib-Ticklers* (which has over 1,000 reviews and 4 stars on Amazon) is an Obvious book. *A Brief History of Time* by Stephen Hawking is a Non-Obvious book. They're both books—but are they the same?

Not even close.

But what about a book like *Don't Reply All: 18 Email Tactics That Help You Write Better Emails and Improve Communication with Your Team*? Which is that "more like?" The joke book? Or a summarization of how the universe began? The answer is: it's Obvious. It's the same as the joke book—except instead of 1001 jokes, it's giving you 18 email tactics.

This is what so many writers and creators misunderstand about monetizing their work.

Whether you write a book, or create a course, or put together a keynote speech, or hold monthly mastermind sessions, bookcamps, or workshops is sort of irrelevant. They're all potential vehicles and they all work (some writers make a lot of money writing books, others make a lot of money selling courses, etc.). When in doubt, we are biased toward choosing digital vehicles over analog vehicles given their ability to scale on the Internet, but it's up to you.

Instead, when trying to find the right monetization vehicles for your Obvious content, these are the two questions you should ask yourself:

Question #1: What type of content do you enjoy creating the most?

This is a personal question.

Which do you enjoy more: writing? Or creating videos? Or do you enjoy doing things in person? Do you get a lot out of "being in the room" with people, and prefer creating things in the physical form? Or do you prefer sitting at home distributing things in the digital world via your laptop or smartphone? Are you an introvert or an extrovert? Do you like getting on planes several times a month to go speak at different industry events? Or does traveling that much give you anxiety (and make you sick)?

The hardest part of being a writer or creator (of any kind) is remaining consistent over a long period of time. Which means it's in your best interest to choose mediums you inherently enjoy and are intrinsically motivated to continue mastering. If you hate writing books, that's going to be a difficult way for you to monetize your Obvious insights, stories, action steps, frameworks, and expertise (and you will never be as successful as another Obvious creator who is absolutely obsessed and in love with writing books). Conversely, if you love doing in-person workshops, then even though you won't ever experience the same scale as an Obvious creator in the digital world, you will likely stick with it longer and become the Category King of your niche—

earning a whole lot more money than if you tried to monetize in a different, less enjoyable way.

So, find the content medium you enjoy most and do that.

A lot.

Question #2: Where are your Superconsumers?

Where are the people you want to help most?

This is where you need to strike a balance between "what you want" and "who you want to reach." For example: if you love creating videos, but are trying to reach writers, then you need to find a way to distribute videos on platforms where writers are (Twitter, LinkedIn, etc.). Conversely, if you love writing online and you are easily reaching the people you want to help most, then you don't need to hop on the newest social media trend and start creating content elsewhere. You don't need to make TikTok videos or start a YouTube channel. You are already reaching your Superconsumers—which means those "other platforms" are more of a distraction than they are a point of leverage.

An easy way of figuring this out is asking yourself what you are a Superconsumer of, yourself.

- Which of these Mediums are you a Super of?
- Are you a Native Analog or Native Digital?
- Where do you "hang out" physically or digitally?
- What sort of relationships do you value most?
- If you wanted to meet more people "like you," where would you go?

Make Your Money While You Can

If you want to make money, achieve credibility, and advance your career in the short term, Obvious content is the place to start. However (going back to our "How much does the party cost?" and "Who is the party for?" questions), if creating Obvious content starts to make you money, and you get used to that newfound credibility and status, and you increase your style of living (you made it!) and burn rate as a result, it will become harder and harder to get off the Obvious content hamster wheel, *transition*, and rise to the next level of The Content Pyramid. You're stuck. You need to keep making money because you need to sustain your lifestyle so you create more and more Obvious content—and round and round you go. (That's why there are over 1,950 *For Dummies* books and counting.)

Because today's desired result won't be tomorrow's desired result.

For example, the mistake all of the authors who've written *For Dummies* books have made is they wrote Obvious insight books, with limited shelf-lives, with someone else's brand name, all of which guarantees no one will remember their name. This is alright if you want short-term success (surely they made a few bucks in the process). But the likelihood this approach leads to any of them becoming a category-leading author with a library that compounds in value is very, very low.

Any and all customers you attract are only as "sticky" as your ability to continue solving new Obvious problems for them. A perfect example is when an Obvious creator launches an email newsletter promising you (the reader) "3 frameworks to solve X, every Monday, Wednesday, and Friday." A lot of writers and creators think the value of a newsletter like this is the fact that they're creating (or receiving) something 3 days per week. That's false. The reader/customer does not care whether they receive 3 emails or 5 emails or 1 email each week. What they care about is solving X. Which means the value of your newsletter is the degree to which you can help the reader/customer solve X problem in their life. AND, your newsletter will only remain valuable *so long as X remains an urgent and important problem in the world.* (There were newsletters in the late 90s and early 2000s helping people learn how to write HTML to create their first website on the Internet. Those newsletters are not "valuable" anymore because the Obvious problem they were solving was replaced by some new, more urgent and more important Obvious problem.)

This is what makes creating Obvious content a bit of a hamster wheel. And if you value your time, this will not be a fun place for you.

Level 4: How To Monetize As A Non-Obvious Creator

Every writer and creator should strive to monetize in all of these different ways—so your income is diversified, and how you "pay for the party" isn't as "fragile."

- You'll want to write books
- And launch courses
- And get hired to speak
- And create digital products
- And maybe launch a paid newsletter
- And hold bootcamps, workshops, and masterminds
- And so on.

It's just a question of sequence.

Both Obvious and Non-Obvious creators can build tremendous careers for themselves. But the big difference between the two comes down to pricing power—and the older you get, the more important this becomes (because your time becomes more precious, which means you want to be able to charge more for your limited time). The difference is that Obvious creators provide products and services. Whereas Non-Obvious creators provide experiences and transformations. And the more valuable the transformation, the more your expertise and insight is valued.

However, not everyone makes the transition from Obvious creator to Non-Obvious creator.

In fact, we find it's more common for Non-Obvious creators to start out as Non-Obvious creators and never bother with Obvious creation at all. They would rather "do their own thing" and wait ten or twenty years (or even their entire lifetime!) for the world to "get" what they believe matters most—than waste time playing the Obvious game for money, status, and short-term impact.

There is no "one right answer" here.

Again, the world needs both: Obvious creators who help you fix urgent problems ("How to fix your dishwasher in 10 minutes or less"), and Non-Obvious creators ("Here's the real reason why capitalism boomed the year dishwashers were invented") help you see the world in new and different ways.

What is interesting, however, is that Non-Obvious creators can also experience massive money and status outcomes, they are just usually delayed. But when they do, that person is cemented in history forever. For decades, Jordan B. Peterson was "just" a professor. A smart one. A talented and respected one. But far from the public figure he is today. That's 30+ years of delayed outcomes—studying, teaching, crystallizing his unique frameworks and "the way he sees the world," until one day, these teachings become "timeless." Peter Drucker, one of the greatest "management" thinkers of all time, was the same way. Drucker has arguably become more famous, and more respected, in the years since his death.

Business Model: Direct-To-Creator for Experiences & Transformations

Both Obvious and Non-Obvious creators can use Direct-To-Creator business models to get paid directly by their readers, listeners, viewers, and customers.

The Achilles' heel for Non-Obvious creators, however, is they usually lack both the competence and the desire to learn about and effectively leverage business models of any kind. That's because Non-Obvious creators would rather spend more of their time, energy, and mental bandwidth focusing on their work—connecting Non-Obvious data points and ideas to reach net-new Non-Obvious conclusions. This is what makes publishing books and other intellectual capital through traditional publishing houses so appealing (as does the decision to "hire a manager"). The publisher takes over responsibility of all the business functions, allowing the Non-Obvious Creator to focus primarily on their work.

But this decision creates a larger "life" problem than most Non-Obvious creators realize.

Non-Obvious creators already don't make as much money (as Obvious creators) in the short term.

When you choose to defer responsibility over the "business" side of your work, particularly when you sign a book deal with a major publisher, you are actively choosing to give up 90% ownership in the asset that was already likely to not make very much money in the short term— but has a good shot at holding its value (or exponentially increasing in value) in the long term. It's Non-Obvious content. It wasn't going to make you much money now anyways. But in signing with a traditional publisher, you give up all your future upside—which is the entire purpose of creating Non-Obvious content in the first place (and why publishers *love, love, love* buying Non-Obvious content for pennies on the dollar a decade before their value is unlocked).

Herein lies the dilemma:

If the "trap" for Obvious creators is making money and achieving status in the short term, and then getting "hooked" on that money/status and remaining on the Obvious content hamster wheel forever, then the "trap" for Non-Obvious creators is trying to capture money and status in the short term for their Non-Obvious work (by signing with a publishing company for an advance to "live on") but giving up 90% of their long-term upside. This is how brilliant, Non-Obvious creators stay poor—or make a decent living, but end up leaving gargantuan amounts of money on the table. When first starting out, they need money to live on "now," but don't want to learn how to use Obvious creation to make that happen for themselves (to fund and fuel their Non-Obvious work), so they sell ownership in their Non-Obvious work long before its value has been realized.

A $100,000 advance for your book sounds great—until 10 years goes by and you realize your publisher has made tens of millions.

In addition, Non-Obvious Creator business models are still Direct-To-Creator, but the portfolio leans less on products (books, courses, etc.) and services (speaking, consulting, advising, etc.), and more on experiences (super premium guru consulting & community-driven courses) and transformations (outcome-based services, digital products, books, advising, etc.).

You might be wondering what the difference is between Q&A consulting, guru consulting, and outcome-based consulting—so here's a quick breakdown:

- **Q&A consulting** is when the questions that are asked are the same questions asked by different people. "How do I cut my costs? How do I market to my customers?" This becomes fairly straightforward with enough experience and can be a great (Obvious) way to monetize, but since the questions are standardized, many people can answer them. Which means your pricing is constrained and tends to be lower. This is the type of consulting most Obvious content creators do. "My 5-how-to-steps" are like everyone else's 5-how-to-steps.
- **Guru consulting** is when your Non-Obvious content is unique and you are known as the only person in the world

who can answer that question. Gurus tend to be quirky and part of the benefit is the experience and entertainment that comes with working with them. Anyone who has worked with Pirate Christopher knows what we mean about the experience (and entertainment) of Pirate Christopher! You're known as the best or the only person who can answer these Non-Obvious questions—and so the market has no other choice but to buy from you.

- **Outcome-based consulting** is when guarantee an outcome (or guarantee you'll get pretty close). That's 7-figure stuff—either cash or equity or both. In addition, there is oftentimes actual scarcity, but at a minimum there must be the perception of scarcity. (For example: if you walk past a really nice restaurant you've heard has great reviews, but when you look inside the window nobody is there, then you're most likely going to keep walking.)

Since Non-Obvious Creators inherently have less volume (fewer shots on goal), by definition they have to charge higher prices for their limited time and volume. Being an expert witness is a great example. A few years ago, Pirate Eddie got a call to see if he would be willing to be an expert witness in a lawsuit related to an acquisition. The company that was acquired had shareholders who believed the acquisition price was far too low and was suing the acquiring company for not paying a higher premium. At the core of the dispute was a valuation model assumption of the category growth rate that drove the discounted cash flow analysis.

Pirate Eddie used a lot of Non-Obvious thinking related to Superconsumers that built a Non-Obvious business case for category growth that defended the purchase price as fair. The best part was Pirate Eddie didn't have to do any of the grunt work. He just had to do the thinking, since there was a team of PhD economists who actually did the analysis and wrote the report to put that together. (The biggest benefit of being a Non-Obvious Creator is your "value" is the thinking, not the doing!) Pirate Eddie was able to charge a small fortune to do that work, largely because there were hundreds of millions of dollars at stake. And it took very little of his time. His Non-Obvious business case was so powerful that the opposition dropped the lawsuit before Pirate Eddie even had his deposition training. (Translation: Non-Obvious thinkers can earn exponential money when the world "gets" the value of their unique intellectual capital.)

And the best Non-Obvious Creators can offer outcome-based consulting. This is when the consultant is almost guaranteeing a certain outcome from the Non-Obvious content and the Obvious or Non-Obvious actions that get executed as a result. Outcomes can be things like "you'll save 20-30% of your procurement cost," which is what AT Kearney became famous for with their strategic sourcing practice, or like exponentially changing the valuation of a company because of its Category Design as they go public. (Another example: the best sales copywriters in the world don't charge per word, or per hour, or even per asset. They charge *per sale* their sales copy facilitates. The outcome they are selling is: "I will write, or rewrite, your sales page, and I am so confident I will increase your sales that I don't want you to pay me any money upfront. But I want 10% of every new sale that comes in, moving forward." Most writers don't know this, but these top-tier sales copywriters make more money than most C-level executives.)

The point is: as a Non-Obvious writer and creator, you will always make the most money when you find ways to monetize the experience, outcome, or transformation and not just "the information." It's like going to Tuscany and having an older Italian couple cook you an authentic Italian dinner. You aren't paying for the ingredients in the meal. You're paying for the meal plus the view of the vineyard plus the impromptu history lesson you receive from the couple while they pour you a glass of wine.

- *Lowest order* = *selling the information*
- *Highest order* = *selling the experience & transformation*

Obvious Income, & Non-Obvious Investments

The ideal scenario for a writer or creator of any kind is to leverage both.

- Obvious content pays for your life in the short term ("Here's how to do it").
- Non-Obvious content pays for your life in the long term ("Here's how to think about it, always and forever").

As a Non-Obvious creator, there is tremendous benefit to creating Obvious content, products, and services to advance your position in life in the short term (giving you income) while simultaneously allowing your long-term bets the decade or two they require to mature (these are your Non-Obvious investments)—and for their value to be realized in the world *without* having to give up 90% ownership out of desperation in the first inning... *aka taking a book deal.*

Pirate Cole's Ship 30 for 30 program is a prime example.

Ship 30 for 30 is a cohort-based writing program for people who want to start writing online. It's a business that educates writers and gives them Obvious frameworks to solve Obvious problems they're experiencing in their lives—everything from overcoming imposter syndrome and procrastination, learning how to start writing on Twitter and LinkedIn, and so on. It is unique. It is differentiated. But at its core, it is Obvious. The business helps people solve urgent problems, and people pay to have those problems solved in actionable, immediate ways. Ship 30 for 30 pays for Pirate Cole's life in the short term.

Whereas this book, and just about everything we publish here at Category Pirates, is Non-Obvious.

It would be foolish to think this Non-Obvious book would grow faster and generate more money, social media attention & status, and short-term impact than something like Ship 30 for 30—because Non-Obvious content doesn't do that. The content in this book is more "thinking," less "doing." As a result, this book is (likely) going to make significantly less money, earn less social media attention and status, and have much less of an impact *in the short term*.

But in the long term?

Our Category Pirates newsletter, and the Non-Obvious framework we are explaining here may remain relevant (and pay dividends) forever—and hopefully inspire a whole generation of "independent" Category-Of-One writers! And having an Obvious business like Ship 30 for 30 is what allows Pirate Cole the freedom to dedicate time to Category Pirates and make long-term, Non-Obvious bets.

Monetizing In Non-Obvious Ways

How you maximize "the value of your value" as a creator is by monetizing Obvious or Non-Obvious content in Non-Obvious ways.

For example, Pirate Christopher's book, *Play Bigger*, is $30. That's a very Obvious business model for selling access to knowledge, and a small price to pay to get to learn directly from some of the fathers of Category Design. However, it's hard to build a fortune off a $30 book—especially when the publisher owns 90% of it (*Play Bigger* was published by Harper Business), and even harder when you have to share the remaining 10% with three other co-authors (*Play Bigger* was also written by Al Ramadan, Dave Peterson, and Kevin Maney). Which means in order for the intellectual capital in *Play Bigger* to be effectively monetized, it would need to "win" the volume game.

It would have to sell millions and millions of copies.

What most people don't know, however, is that 99% of the insight and information in *Play Bigger* is the same insight Pirate Christopher gets paid (in cash and equity) by startups to explain individually to them—helping companies design and dominate a new category of consequence. This is a Non-Obvious way of monetizing the same information. And as Pirate Christopher likes to say, "That's the reason I don't have a mortgage." Same information, same insight and knowledge, different business model. Pirate Christopher doesn't need millions and millions of entrepreneurs buying his knowledge for $30. He needs one entrepreneur of one high-potential startup to "buy" his intellectual capital and give him equity in the company in exchange for helping apply knowledge and facilitate a transformation in the business. (Pirate Eddie uses this same business model, as does Pirate Cole, because it's an incredibly effective way to multiply the value of your value. This is what we call being an Intellectual Capitalist: someone who turns thinking into value that didn't exist before.)

Low volume, extremely high price.

So, here's the framework:

To increase the value of your value, make "access" more private, exclusive, and personal.

If you want to read Pirate Cole's insights on digital writing, you can buy his book, *The Art & Business of Online Writing* for $20.

Or, if you want to learn these frameworks, writing techniques, and distribution strategies from Pirate Cole directly in a group setting, you can join Ship 30 for 30 for $500.

Or, if you want Pirate Cole to give you individual and personalized feedback on your writing, you can schedule a "Power Hour" with him for $1,000.

Or, if you want Pirate Cole to be your private ghostwriter, you can be one of his select clients and work with him directly for $20,000 per month.

Or, if you want Pirate Cole to ghostwrite/co-author your book, you can hire him for $250,000.

Or, if you want Pirate Cole to create the languaging and messaging strategy for your startup, you can hire him for 0.5% equity in the company.

What most people don't realize is that almost all of the information that is in Pirate Cole's $20 book is much of the same information he shares in all of the other ways he monetizes—except with more access. Just like how most of Pirate Christopher's mental models and high-level frameworks on Category Design are in his book, *Play Bigger*, but Silicon Valley startups still want to hire him directly. And just like how Pirate Eddie's entire Superconsumer framework is laid out in his book, *Superconsumers*, but Fortune 500 companies still want Eddie to walk them through the process and hold their hand.

To increase the "value of your value," the key is to make access to you and your specialized knowledge more private and personal. Your book can be $20 but your pre-recorded online course (explaining the same information) can be $200. Why? Because now the reader/listener/customer can see your face. They can hear your vocal inflections, and gain access to the spontaneous stories and insights you might have forgotten (or chose not to) include in your book. **They feel closer to you, and get a different level of experience as a result.** And when you teach those same concepts live, on Zoom, you can (and should) charge more—because you're providing a different, more "valuable" experience. And when you teach those same concepts or tell those same stories privately for a small group of select people, you can (and should) charge more—because you're providing a different, more "valuable" experience. And so on.

The information isn't really what's changing.

It's the way it's being presented and personalized—increasing the level of direct access the audience has with you.

Level 5: How To Monetize As
A Category Creator

The apex of The Content Pyramid is to become a Category Creator. This means you have successfully become known for a niche you own, and that niche has a tailwind behind it (that you have either created or accelerated) that will last long enough for you to exceed your "burn rate," save and invest money, create and buy assets that pay you dividends long into the future, have a meaningful impact on the world, achieve a level of status that ensures new opportunities continue to fall into your lap, and allow you to do what you love every single day until the day your life comes to an end.

Pure creative joy.

If this sounds like a pipe dream, we're here to tell you it's not. We live this pure creative joy every single day. We love working on Category Pirates. We're grateful to have the legendary opportunities we have in our work—as writers and beyond writing. And our "soul goal" in sharing our learnings with you is we want you to thrive and experience this creative joy too. We think the world needs more creative/innovative people like you to make a legendary living doing legendary work.

And we hope your takeaway here is that it's possible.

If you've made it this far, then it should be apparent that both Obvious and Non-Obvious Creators can become Category Creators. However, Obvious Category Creators typically become known for niches with shorter shelf lives, and may need to hop from Obvious category to Obvious category several times to remain relevant throughout their career. Non-Obvious Category Creators, on the other hand, take longer to establish themselves (they are usually building a new niche/category from scratch) but remain relevant longer than their Obvious counterparts.

The real test as to whether you have transcended and become a true Category Creator really comes down to one single question:

"What is your category?"

If you ask 100 people this question, 100 of them should all say the exact same thing.

To show how this works, there is a session in Ship 30 for 30 where Pirate Cole asks the cohort of writers, "What is Ryan Holiday's category?" And within 3 seconds, every writer in the Zoom chat writes one word, over and over again.

- Stoicism
- Stoicism
- Stoicism
- Stoicism
- Stoicism
- Stoicism
- Stoicism
- Stoicism

This is the test.

(Ryan's first several books were on completely different topics. But when his "Stoicism" work started to tip, he went all in and continued writing about Stoicism until he eventually became known for this niche—which he now owns.)

If and when it becomes crystal clear (as a result of your work, your contributions to the category, and your consistent output over a long period of time) what 1-2-3-4 words summarize your category, and 100 out of 100 people all say those same exact words when describing you, you win.

And the reason you win is because once this happens, nobody can step into your category without immediately being compared to you.

"You write about Stoicism? That's cool—you're like Ryan Holiday!"

Business Model: Category King Economics

According to our research, Category King economics states that Category Creators capture 76% of the market capitalization of their category. In layman's terms, this means that when you are the Category King (of any category or niche, big or small), you are the one who benefits the most from that category's growth. For example, if Ryan Holiday is the undisputed Category King of the Stoicism education category, then the more Stoicism as a category grows in popularity, out of all the writers and thinkers who write about Stoicism, Ryan Holiday is going to be the one who benefits the most. He's going to capture the majority of the upside (76%) while all the other wanna-be Ryan Holidays fight over the remaining 24% (forever stuck in "The Better Trap").

Why?

Because who was writing about Stoicism on a practical level before Ryan Holiday wrote *The Obstacle Is The Way* in 2014? Nobody. And who else has published more books, content, and educational media on the subject of Stoicism since? Nobody. The moment you type "Stoicism" into Google, YouTube, Facebook, Instagram, Twitter, TikTok, Medium, Quora, or any other meaningful digital platform, you either immediately discover Ryan Holiday, or you discover thousands of writers writing about Stoicism and referencing Ryan Holiday's work.

He won—that category.

Because he created/redesigned it.

The only way Ryan Holiday loses dominance over the Stoicism category is by:

- **Abandoning It.** Maybe after another 10 years he'll decide he's made his money and is no longer interested in writing about Stoicism. But even still, he will likely remain known for this niche—and as long as interest in his category remains relevant, so will his work (until someone comes along and changes the definition of the category).

- **Being "Niched Down."** Ryan Holiday is known for Stoicism, but how he loses his foothold is if another creator comes along and creates a new, even larger category in which Stoicism is just one "niche." But even still, as long as Stoicism as a niche remains relevant, so will Ryan Holiday (see the power of being a Category King?).
- **The Big Brand Lie.** The other thing that could happen (which happens to many legendary creators once they achieve a certain level of success) is they fall for The Big Brand Lie. They forget that what made them successful was their new unique category—not "them" and their "personal brand." (People know who Ryan Holiday is because of his contributions to the Stoicism category, not because his name is Ryan Holiday.) Once this happens, the writer/creator stops evangelizing their category and starts promoting themselves. Their name on their books gets bigger and bigger. Their social media content becomes less about their category and more about "them." Until, all of a sudden, the writer/creator has completely stopped nurturing their category—leaving an opportunity for some other writer or creator to come along and pick up where they left off. So, pretty please (with rum on top), don't fall for The Big Brand Lie!

Categories make creators, not the other way around.

When you become known for a niche you own, you solidify your career.

You don't have to worry about being "knocked off." (The more people try to knock you off, the more they reinforce your Category King position!)

You don't have to worry about not having any income in the future. (As long as your category remains relevant, and you continue to evangelize and promote its importance, you will thrive as a writer & creator.)

And most of all, you don't have to fight for demand in other people's categories. (You stand alone.)

Legendary Writer, No Category Design

What is Malcolm Gladwell's category?

You know he's a legendary writer, but what's his category called?

If you asked 100 people to name Malcolm Gladwell's category, would they all say the same 1-2-3-4 words? (Ryan Holiday's is "Stoicism." What's Gladwell's?)

The fact that you don't know (and we don't know) is a bigger problem than most writers and creators realize. You see, it's amazing to be a legendary writer and Obvious or Non-Obvious creator, but what separates Category Creators is the languaging they've attached to their category. You know exactly who they are and what they write about in a single sentence—sometimes even a single word (Stoicism). When this happens, word-of-mouth marketing catches fire. All you have to do is say 1 or 2 words and you can summarize what "that writer" is, does, and writes about. But how do you explain why someone should read Malcolm Gladwell?

"Well... what he does is he tells these stories... and they're all sort of disconnected... and they're really great... basically he's a non-fiction writer who... well it's all correlated..."

It's much harder for word-of-mouth marketing to spark when 100 out of 100 of your readers don't have the same language to educate the world about who you are, what you write about, and why it matters.

Whereas, if someone wanted to tell you to read Ryan Holiday, all they'd have to say is:

"Oh, you should read his work. He writes about Stoicism."

This is very important—and even easier to see in the world of fiction:

There are a gazillion "thriller" writers in the world.

So the way you "stand out" isn't by making your name on the book cover a bigger font than everyone else. (This might sound ridiculous but this is *actually* the strategy publishers use and think is best.)

The way you "stand out" is by using languaging to change the category.

Better to be King of a different category than a peasant of a broad, saturated category.

- "You should read John Grisham. He writes **Legal Thrillers.**"
- "You should read Stephen King. He writes **Supernatural Thrillers.**"
- "You should read Agatha Christie. She writes **Detective Thrillers.**"
- "You should read Lee Child. He writes **Military Thrillers.**"

It's not you, or your "passion for writing" that you are promoting.

It's the different word you are using to describe what makes your category new & different. ("It's not a thriller. It's a Military Thriller!")

Which means your job—as a writer, but also as the marketer behind your movement—is to put "the right words" in "the right mouths."

That's how you get people to talk about you and your work, solidify your Category King position, and build a legendary career that "pays for your party" for the rest of your life.

CHAPTER THREE

Content-Free Marketing:

How Marketers Got Duped Into Saying Nothing, Everywhere (And Why It Is A Legendary Opportunity)

Now let's talk about marketing.

The content marketing category is a $400 billion industry. And it's estimated that by 2024, the content marketing industry will grow by another $270 billion, bringing the grand total to nearly $700 billion.

But "content marketing" is broad, and includes everything from creation to distribution to content management. For example, in 2020 the enterprise content management industry was valued at $47 billion, and is projected to more than double over the next five years to more than $105 billion. Translation: of the soon-to-be $700 billion content marketing industry, 20% of the entire market is exclusively dedicated to "managing" the content that gets created.

Well, what's the content?

More importantly, how much of the content being created (especially by enterprise companies and B2C companies) is actually worth reading? When was the last time you clicked on a company blog post, opened a company newsletter, or listened to a corporate podcast and said to yourself, "Wow, I sure am glad I clicked on that!" The fact that most content marketing is garbagé (as they say in French) represents one of the greatest marketing opportunities of our time—for those willing to buck current conventional wisdom.

The "content management" subcategory of the mega content marketing category is growing faster than ever—and yet, according to Content Hacker, the #1 activity B2B companies outsource is content creation (by a mile). **86% of B2B organizations surveyed said they outsourced content creation.** The next-closest activity is content distribution, which only 30% of B2B organizations surveyed said they did. Editorial planning, 11%. Content strategy, 10%. Content technology, 10%. And so on.

Now let's connect these two data points.

- On the one hand, "content management" is growing at breakneck speed. Content creation creates more to manage.

- On the other hand, "content creation" is often the number one most outsourced marketing activity. Which means companies are deferring the single most important aspect of "content," which is the creation of each and every idea.

And who is coming up with the ideas?

As we wrote about in our mini-book, *The "Me" Disease*, many marketers today have (unfortunately) caught Gary Vee-D, a "content disease" that leads creators and companies alike to believe the whole purpose of content creation is to "do it"—and to do it as often as possible. Document everything, right? It doesn't matter if it's good. It doesn't matter if it's valuable. Just say it loud and say it often. "Pump out 200 pieces of content a day!" Gary Vee and other digital marketing shysters have led the masses to believe the fact you "did it" means you are succeeding. More equals mo' better. You are winning. And so marketers everywhere have adopted this Spray & Pray approach—where 100% of the emphasis is on the output, and essentially 0% (OK, that might be a slight exaggeration, but you get the point) of the emphasis is on the quality of the content and what's actually being said.

As a result, creators and enterprises deploy "more content, more often" strategies.

Again: of the soon-to-be $700 billion content marketing industry, 20% of the entire market is exclusively dedicated to "managing" the content that gets created. The other 80% gets outsourced to agencies, contractors, analysts, and "gurus" whose "big idea" is to get you to post quote graphics from yourself (or your company) on LinkedIn 12x per day with things like, "Hustle is the secret to success" and "Win small, to win big."

This is what we like to call content-free marketing.

Content-Free Marketing: The Art Of Saying Nothing, Everywhere

In our mini-book, *The Lightning Strike Strategy*, we wrote about how advertising legends of old (like David Ogilvy) were not successful because of Reach & Frequency strategies. Reach & Frequency means "the more people (reach) who see my brand, more often (frequency), the better off we'll be." No, these advertising legends were successful because they owned a specific position in the customer's mind (a category).

Our friend and teacher, Silicon Valley's secret attack marketing sensei Rick Bennett's mindset is (we're paraphrasing) "If these marketing dollars are the last dollars a company has, how do we create one ad, or a quick strike, that will *make* the company—in *one* marketing move." He's done this many times. One of our favorites is the "I will not give my lunch money to Siebel" ad, which helped Marc Benioff's Salesforce.com underscore the cost advantage of Cloud Computing over Client/Server.

This is the opposite of Spray and Pray. This content, based on a radically different Point-of-View, is designed to make a very big impact—with *one* strike. And it's engineered to get people talking about what makes you *different*, all in an effort to make your POV *stick* and become *their* different too. Remember, legendary category marketing empowers word of mouth. Which means the way you think about "content creation" that has the potential to "make" you and/or your company should follow this blueprint:

1. **What's your POV?** What are you actually saying? Which direction are you leading people's thinking? (If you are leading them in the same direction as everyone else, you are part of the noise. The only way to not be part of the noise is to, quite literally, *not* say the same thing and *not* lead their thinking in the same direction.)

2. **What is the transformation as a result of adopting this POV?** When someone follows your line of thinking, where do they end up? Jerusalem? Or a real-estate flipping seminar in the basement of a church in Las Vegas? Do they experience a plastic-y, incremental outcome, or an

exponential one? On a scale of 1 to 10, how DIFFERENT is their life (and/or business) before & after listening to, digesting, and internalizing your new POV?

3. **How can you get your Superconsumers to hear & adopt your POV?** Enabling the most influential people in your category to evangelize your POV is the fastest path to enduring, exponential growth. Which means your primary focus should NOT be to get "anyone" to hear your POV, but to leverage the attention and enthusiasm of your Superconsumers. Your job is to put the right words (your POV) in the right mouths (your Supers, which we'll talk about how to do in a bit).

It's estimated that, back in the 70s, the average person saw between 500 and 1,600 ads per day. By 2007, that number had climbed up to 5,000 ads per day. And in 2021, it's now estimated "the average person encounters between 6,000 and 10,000 ads every single day." This includes the brand of camera you use as your webcam, the logo on the coffee mug on your desk, the name on your T-shirt, and so on.

Now add a billion "content-free" social media posts on top of that.

- "Follow your passion!"
- "Data is the future!"
- "You have to love yourself, first!"
- "Authentic leadership is the best kind of leadership!"
- "Companies have to care about culture!"

All of these content-free POVs are noise. And just like how companies fall for The Big Brand Lie, thinking the key to building a successful business is to push your brand further, faster, and more often than everyone else, companies and marketers and entire content marketing departments fall for The Big Content Lie, thinking what matters most isn't what the content is saying—but whether or not "whatever" is being said is seen by the most people, most often.

The business world has created a Content Marketing Industrial Complex (and doesn't even know it).

A content marketing department supply chain looks like this:

- You come up with an idea for a piece of content
- You write the content
- You edit the content
- You manage the writing and editing of the content
- You post the content
- You ask other people to post the content
- You pay to boost/promote the content
- You pay other people to post, share, and backlink to the content
- You manage the posting, and the sharing, and the backlinking of the content
- And then you count up how many views, Likes, comments, shares, backlinks, and (maybe) sales the content accumulated.

Only 1 of those steps is about the quality of the content (your differentiated POV).

The other 9 steps are about the amplification of the content (which means, if you don't have a differentiated POV to begin with, what are the other 9 steps even in service of? More for more's sake?). For example, we know people in the podcasting category who have between 70-80% audience churn. As a result, they spend increasing amounts of time, money, and technology on "new listener acquisition." Which they do to keep their download numbers up so they can continue charging their sponsorship rates.

Instead of working on creating a radically different POV within a radically different category design as a strategy for growth, these creators simply pour more gas on their content-free marketing dumpster fire. We see exactly the same mentality in marketing organizations. More content for more lead generation, more funnels to catch more prospects with more content, more content for more lead nurture, and so on. MORE CONTENT is the "answer" at every stage of the "customer journey."

The business world has unknowingly created this Content Marketing Industrial Complex because "such a complex is said to pursue its own financial interests regardless of, and often at the expense of, the best interests of society and individuals." For example, how do Content Management Platforms make money? They need customers who have a problem called: "I have too much content to manage." The CMS market is valued at $62 billion. Within that market are startups like Content-stack, which in 2021 raised a $57.5 million Series B. These companies make up a category that is both the problem and the solution. The problem is, "We have too much content." The solution is, "Use our platform to manage *even more* content." And on and on the Content Marketing Industrial Complex grows, where "The industrial complex may profit financially from maintaining socially detrimental or inefficient systems," according to Wikipedia's definition of an Industrial Complex.

But that's just the tip of the iceberg.

Since social media is "free" to use, with the potential to reach hundreds of millions of potential readers, listeners, viewers, and even customers, the marketing world has come to believe that mindless output is the secret to "free content marketing."

But is "free content marketing" really free?

First of all, note all the steps that go into managing a company's Content Marketing Industrial Complex. The labor resources (contractors and full-time employees), in addition to enterprise software costs, are not rounding errors. Remember, nearly $700 billion is going to be spent on content marketing by 2025. Couldn't companies find a better way to allocate those precious resources than waste it on more stuff people don't want to consume and/or wish they hadn't? Wouldn't it be better to return that money to shareholders so they could invest it more wisely? (If Wall Street were smart, they would ask on earnings calls how much a company spends on content marketing and then discount their valuation based on that! *ARRRRRRR!*)

Second, while you may not be paying for it or charging your readers or customers money to consume your content, you are charging them *time.* You are costing them emotional disappointment when they realize they spent those precious minutes consuming something with empty calories, or watching you interview a customer hoping to learn about the future of the category but really hearing a disguised testimonial about why they love your new carbadigulator. (*"Well Jim, we believe in the power of The Cloud and A.I. to digitally transform key parts of our business. Our key learning since we started is that this is a journey, not a destination, and to be successful in the new digital world, you've got to take small steps along the way."*)

This is not "content."

It's drivel.

When content marketers do this, they teach readers, listeners, viewers, and potential customers (and investors) to stop paying attention to them.

The customers you care about (your Superconsumers) aren't stupid, and they know regurgitations when they hear them.

The marketing landscape has conflated activities and outcomes.

Lastly, content-free marketing leads to easier, faster, cheaper output. Output is noticeable. Output makes it look like the marketing department is doing something. "Don't you think our new whitepaper, YouTube video, blog post, and podcasts are awesome? Don't you, Sally!?"

Easier, faster, cheaper output leads to more to manage ("Did we already say, 'Hustle is what separates the winners from the losers? Maybe this time we should say, 'Real winners hustle.' Looks like we need to upgrade our Content Management System! We've got a lot to manage!). More to manage means less resources available to create differentiated, fresh, quality content.

Less resources for creating quality content (and/or increased outsourcing of content creation) leads to more content-free marketing. (How did the solution to the problem "our content marketing results are not great" become MORE CONTENT!?)

And on and on the Content Marketing Industrial Complex hairball keeps rolling and growing.

...but stick with us, because in this madness is a giant opportunity for a pirate like you.

Obvious Lie Marketing

- In 2020, the SEO industry was valued at $80 billion.
- The PR industry, $88 billion.
- Social media management industry, $14 billion.

If you are a founder, executive, investor, or small business owner and you've ever hired an SEO firm, a PR firm, or a social media agency, how good are they at coming up with compelling ideas? Most are not. Their job is basically to create content-free content and pump it into algorithms, spam email it to journalists, and pitch it anywhere and everywhere they can—with the hopes of getting a backlink or two to the other content-free content on your website.

Emails and social media posts created in the context of this "strategy" (if we can even call it that) are literally saying, "We are spraying our crap everywhere. Do you like it?"

But this is only the beginning.

One of the great "content marketing hacks" is what we like to call "Obvious Lie Marketing."

Gary Vee wrote a book about it, called *Jab, Jab, Jab, Right Hook: How To Tell Your Story In A Noisy Social World.*

The book, and the coinciding strategy, is to quite literally pretend to "provide value" a few times before hitting the reader, viewer, or listener with your ask. (And when you make your ask, add in an "obvious lie" to make it sound more "authentic".)

On social media, this means posting a couple "inspiring" quote graphics—"Don't Pay Attention To The Haters. They're Just Jealous."—before making your pitch: "Hey #HustleTribe! Just wanted to say HAPPY MONDAY and that today only I'll be selling my Zero-To-Authentic course for 50% off!"

Via cold email, this means opening with something like: "Hey there, Christopher! I just wanted to say how much I enjoyed your most recent episode of *Follow Your Different.* Your podcast is really something special. I loved your most recent episode with <Insert name of last guest on the podcast here>. Anyways, I just wanted to see if you had any interest in hosting one of my content-free blogs on your website? Totally free, of course."

And on company blogs, this means being very deliberate about not including anything "too valuable" in the free blog post (remember, the secret to content-free marketing is for the content to not be where the REAL value is—you have to pay for that!) and instead use the "free" blog post as bait to force readers to give you their email, subscribe to your newsletter, or enter your funnel. Bonus points if, after they've subscribed, they find even more content-free content. The best newsletters are written by underpaid interns, after all.

The majority of marketers have internalized all of the above, as well as the belief that the best way to "build relationships" with readers, listeners, viewers, and potential customers is to start off by flattering them (with Obvious Lies), motivating them, fluffing them up a bit ("authentically," of course), and then whacking them over the head. (BANG! POW! ZONK!) But what you're really saying when you do this is, "Hey there. I think you're stupid. And I think you're going to fall for this stupid ploy of garbagé content wrapped in disngenuous complements."

You are beginning the relationship with an insult to the reader's intelligence.

(And somehow this became an accepted "best practice" in marketing.)

When you stop and take the time to look, it's astonishing how much of the content world is valueless—and *at the exact same time*, how many people run around preaching, "You have to provide value! Don't forget to provide value! Content is king! Be authentic!" (*Ever notice how many of the marketing experts who talk about authenticity come across as deeply inauthentic?*)

By the looks of it, most content marketers don't have a clue what that even means.

But they heard some social media guru say it (120 times), so it must be right.

The 3 Big Content Marketing Lies (And The Massive Opportunity They Create)

If you wouldn't pay for it—either with hours or dollars—why are you putting it out?

If it's not legendary, why are you doing it?

(As soon as you change the mindset from "legendary volume" to "legendary content," you will stand out.)

Whenever we challenge people on this topic, *especially* in the context of large enterprise companies (where the entire measure for success is just getting the damn thing done and the report completed before Christmas), we tend to hear two responses:

The first is, "Legendary is a high bar to set! Don't you think that's unreasonable?"

Playing in the NBA is a high bar. Getting into MIT or Juilliard is a high bar. Becoming a doctor is a high bar. How come having millions and millions of people read your work, or listen to your podcast, or watch your YouTube video—and more importantly, *becoming customers and spending money with your company*—isn't a high bar? Where does this entitlement come from?

We'll tell you: it comes from the fact that a) everyone consumes marketing, so everyone considers themselves a marketer, b) social media is free to use, email is free to use, all these digital marketing mechanisms are (on the surface) "free," which severely lowers the barrier to entry, and c) seeing teenagers go viral for doing a 15-second dance or eating a bunch of Tide liquid laundry detergent pods leads the world to believe, "Oh, going viral isn't hard. See? That teenager just did it and what they're doing is stupid."

But...

a) Not everyone is a marketer, let alone any good at it. Just because someone is "in marketing" or their job title says "Senior Marketing Director" doesn't mean the decisions they're making out in the market are smart or making a difference.

b) Social media is easy to use and incredibly difficult to master. There's a low barrier to entry, but a very high skill gap between the top 1% and the other 99%.

c) Viral is not, and should not be your goal. (Everyone slows down to gawk at the car accident on the side of the road but that doesn't mean you should crash your car.) Anyone can go viral, and the vast majority of the time it happens by accident. "Getting lucky" should not be your core strategy. Remember: no one owes you their attention.

The second is, "Sometimes we just have to get things done."

Sure, we get that.

Us pirates tend to err on the side of "getting things done" versus "not getting things done" as well.

The strategic question is *what* are we getting done?

These scenarios should be few and far between. Meaning: in a year, the number of times you have to make the decision, "Ah you know what? This is good enough. Let's just hit publish and move on," should be minimal. If it happens, and you've gotta do it, then we agree: it's better to take an imperfect step than to not take a step at all.

But when this becomes your dominant state, you've got a problem. Because now you are building a process, and a "content supply chain," optimized for mediocrity.

Don't confuse the activity with the results.

We believe the reason people have beliefs like "That's a high bar to set" or "Sometimes we just have to get things done" is because there are 3 big lies actively perpetuated throughout the content marketing world—and these lies trick people into thinking that marketing is easy. Anyone can do it. Worst of all, the key to great content marketing isn't to focus on the quality of the content (the idea, the POV) but the marketing, the distribution, the posting schedule, *the management of the content*, and so on.

Newsflash: what *time of day* you post your content is IRRELE-VANT (*ARRRRRR!!!!!!!*) if what you're posting is content-free.

Lie #1: "The most valuable form of marketing is your personal story."

Go anywhere on the Internet and you'll see this lie being spread at an unprecedented scale.

In a marketing group, we recently saw a "marketer" give this advice to other "marketers," explaining that the best way to promote their startup is to share their startup's journey.

Unfortunately, there's a nuance missing here, and it's a big one. Which is: ONLY IF YOU CAN TRANSLATE YOUR JOURNEY INTO SOMETHING THAT MATTERS TO YOUR CUSTOMERS.

Because no one cares about you.

For example, let's say the three of us started a real estate consulting business where we worked with Airbnb owners scaling their portfolios of rental properties. A typical marketer would say, "The best way to promote your business is to share your own personal story."

Alright, here goes.

> *"Hey guys! Happy Tuesday. Just wanted to let you know that today we landed another 3 clients. Awesome, huh? Yea, so things are going pretty well here at Pirate, Pirate & Pirate Real Estate Incorporated. Stay tuned for tomorrow—and don't forget to HUSTLE!"*

How effective is this at getting your Superconsumers to give you their undivided attention?

(It's not.)

Now, instead of focusing on our personal story, let's try this again but make our target customer and their story, their wants and needs and desires the priority.

*"Happy Tuesday, Airbnb owners! You know what time it is. Every Tuesday, we show **you** a rental property we think is undervalued, explain why, and then walk **you** through the different ways **you** could increase the value of this sort of rental property within **your** own portfolio. Fixing just a few of these small things can immediately increase the value of **your** properties, and we want to make sure **you** learn everything **you** need to know to maximize **your** real estate returns. And if anything about this video & walkthrough guide is confusing to **you**, just drop us a comment and we'll add a separate Q&A section to the guide."*

There is a cataclysmic-sized gap between these two examples. The first one is focused on *me, me, me,* and the second is focused on *YOU, YOU, YOU.*

Now, does this mean you shouldn't share anything personal, ever? Of course not. What matters—whether you are creating for yourself or on behalf of your company—is that any personal stories, anecdotes, or details you use *are in support of your mission to educate, empower, and even entertain the reader, viewer, listener, and/or customer.* **They have to be the main character of the story.** If they're not, then you've caught The Me Disease, and your entire strategy is predicated on people thinking you (or your company) is awesome, and choosing to give you their attention (and money) because they think you've got something they don't.

This is a mercenary mindset.

Lie #2: "Anything I say is valuable."

This is a huge issue Pirate Cole ran into with his ghostwriting agency. Highly successful entrepreneurs, executives, investors, and even Olympic athletes and Grammy-winning musicians would sign on looking to position themselves as thought leaders, only to show up to their call and basically have nothing to say. "How do you become an effective leader? Well, you have to be authentic, that's for sure. And you have to motivate your team. And you've got to show up with a good attitude." *Groundbreaking stuff, Tom. Remarkable.*

The problem here is that individuals and companies who have achieved nearly any level of success in their careers begin to drink their own rum and assume everyone should pay attention to them because of what they've achieved. What they fail to realize, however, is that "playing basketball" and articulating how to play basketball are two completely different skills. (There's a reason why Michael Jordan is considered one of the worst basketball franchise owners in history.)

Pirate Eddie ran into the same thing among professionals paid to be "thought leaders." After a few years of writing for *Harvard Business Review*, he would regularly get asked by other consulting partners, executives, and business gurus for help getting an article published in HBR. He would share the formula he had worked out with his editor years ago: a) have a provocative point of view that overturns conventional wisdom, b) back it up with robust data or compelling case studies, and c) draw broadly applicable insights and implications that are useful for as wide of an audience as possible across multiple industries.

Most often, Pirate Eddie would get blank stares back and a response that basically said, "...Ummm, I just want to be published in HBR. Can't you just help me do that?"

That was the response from people *paid handsomely* to have a point of view.

So why was this the case?

It's not that they weren't smart—just like it's not that content marketers aren't smart. It was often more that they didn't have enough courage to say something different. Was this because they were cowards? No. It almost always came back to incentives. They had little to gain by advocating for a different point of view, but felt they had a lot to lose if the world (or their partners or boss) didn't agree. (Standing out means standing alone.) As a result, the vast majority of the "thought leaders" you find in the business world tend to resemble a Marriott lobby. It looks "nice." It's "professional." But the entire design strategy is to be as unremarkably "pleasant" as possible. As a result, they are completely uninteresting, totally forgettable, and radically undifferentiated.

We know the CEO of a major publicly traded tech company who wanted to start a weekly podcast but was stopped by their legal department and board for fear this CEO might say, "The wrong thing."

Meanwhile: Elon Musk, one of the richest and most influential people in the world, is on Twitter posting Memes trolling Bill Gates.

In contrast: one of the first HBR pieces Pirate Eddie wrote after leaving his consulting firm was about why General Mills should sell its cereal business. The thesis (the DIFFERENT POV) was that the cereal category had declined $4 billion over 15 years. And unless leadership believed carbs and sugar were ever coming back in a big way, the cereal business would never be more valuable than it is today. But the reality was no executive wanted to be the one who sold off the cereal business on his or her watch. So, free from the shackles of the "don't-piss-anyone-off police" inside a major consulting firm, Pirate Eddie had the freedom to write that piece—whereas saying something this "different" would have been very difficult back at The Cambridge Group (where Pirate Eddie used to work), which was owned by Nielsen at the time, both of which had strong incentives not to rock the boat.

The PR world and the Content-Free Marketing Industrial Complex has led people to believe that the key to "being seen as a thought leader" is just to be seen. ("Hi guys it's me!") It's not to actually provide differentiated thinking. It's not to say things other people aren't comfortable saying (yet). It's not to push conversations into uncharted territory. It's not to move a category *from* the way it is *to* a new and different way. It's to spew advice like, "The key to being a great leader is authenticity" as often as possible. (A grand slam home run is if the "thought leader's" advice then gets shared in a Tier 2 business publication like *Forbes* or *The Huffington Post*.)

And the reason we believe this has become such a commonly accepted "strategy" for companies and their executives is because spewing undifferentiated thinking across 27 different platforms, costly as it might be, is the only way for a company to say *anything* without flagging HR, legal, the board, and a room full of executives. And so, after all the red tape, a company has said nothing, everywhere, successfully.

This is Content-Free Marketing.

And it is a huge problem. (As well as a massive, legendary opportunity for anyone with a couple brain cells and a willingness to be different.)

Lie #3: "It's all about how many people see my content."

No, it's not.

It's about how many people are moved by your content enough to *share* it.

And not just shares as a blanket metric, but shares specifically amongst your Superconsumers. If you get 1,000,000 views and zero engagement or shares from your Superconsumers, guess what? That's not a very good piece of content. But if you get 10,000 views and 1,000 die-hard enthusiasts of your category are sharing your content like crazy, now you're onto something.

Views, Likes, and follows are vanity metrics. Anyone can get views. The three of us Pirates watch stuff all the time we don't really care about. It hooks our attention for a fleeting moment, and then it's gone and we think nothing of it (videos of cats and raging Karens inside Wal-Mart come to mind). In general, views are a meaningless metric.

Shares, on the other hand, represent someone's identity. When you share something on Facebook or Twitter or Instagram or Pinterest, whatever it is you are "sharing" is speaking for you. It's one deviation away from you creating something on your own. (Shares are why the Net Promoter Score (NPS) works so well, because it requires you to put your own reputation on the line.) And the reason people share certain things online is usually because that piece of content is successfully saying something they weren't able to say themselves. For example: "This sums up how I feel perfectly" is a common caption people use when sharing content.

And the Reach & Frequency you want is not the kind you pay for, or that happens by accident.

You want to earn it.

The goal of your content is not for people to *view* it. Or to Like it.

Your goal is for people to lose their minds over it.

Bookmark it. Share it. Email it to three friends with the subject line: "READ THIS ASAP." You want to get to the point where readers are *actively waiting* for your next piece of content, your next blog post, newsletter, YouTube video, or podcast episode. Your content should be so radically differentiated (aka: provide such new, valuable, differentiated THINKING) that you get emails from worried Supers saying, "Ummm, hi? Just checking in here. It's been two weeks since you posted anything and I'm starting to go through withdrawals. Any update on when the next piece of content is dropping?" (*We have heard from quite a few pirates this is how they feel about our weekly mini-books. And when one arrives, they close up shop for the day, grab a cold one from the fridge, close the door, and read the entire thing—start to finish. This is the greatest compliment in the world to us—ARRRRRRR!!!!!!!*)

Now, if you read the above and are saying to yourself, "Yea OK guys, but that sounds like a lot of work," we're sorry to say you have caught a bad case of Gary Vee-D. (Our deepest condolences... Maybe spray some Windex on it?)

Somewhere along the way, marketing folks internalized the faulty belief that *people owed them their attention.* As a result, you don't have to work for it, and you don't have to put time and attention and tender love and care into the things you create. All you have to do is *document, pump out, record, publish, rah-rah, hustle, kerplow.*

Do Not Confuse Strategy With Tactics

The last thing we want to point out here is the misunderstanding content marketers (and the companies who hire them) have between "strategy" and "tactics."

To put it simply:

- **Strategy** = Which direction are you facing (are you going North or are you going South)?
- **Tactics** = Once you know which direction you're facing, how are you going to get there (by plane, by bus, by boat)?

What time of day you post your content is a *tactic.* Whether you should create videos or blog posts is a *tactic.* Articles like, "How To Use Twitter For Business: 15 Tips To Promote Your Brand" are full of *tactics.* "Engage people with large audiences; Use Twitter lists to manage your feed; target popular hashtags," *ticky-tack-tactics.*

But these tactics have nothing to do with your strategy.

And your strategy has everything to do with what you are actually saying.

The reason the content marketing world is obsessed with tactics is because tactics are easy. "What's the one button I have to press in order for my content to be successful? What's the new hack?" And it's a whole lot easier for some social media guru to tell you how crucial it is for you to post at 3:00 p.m. instead of 4:00 p.m. What's hard is actually sitting there and thinking about the premise of the conversation being had in your category. Do you agree or disagree with the conventional wisdom? How come? And how did you arrive at your conclusion? Is this conclusion new and different in any way? If not, start over and try again.

Strategy is, quite literally, which direction your thinking is facing—and as a result, which direction you are leading the thinking of your readers, viewers, listeners, and customers. If you are "thinking" in the same direction as everyone else, you're noise. You're an inconvenient scroll. And yet, going back to how we started this chapter: 86% of B2B organizations surveyed said they outsource content creation.

They are outsourcing the most important part of the entire "content" supply chain: the nucleus, the red-hot center, *the BIG idea.*

Which is why, when most companies and executives set out in search of content writers, they are often disappointed. Because they aren't actually looking for a content writer or a ghostwriter.

What they're really looking for is a ghost-*thinker.*

And differentiated thinking isn't a commodity you can easily find on Upwork.

A Legendary Opportunity: Saying More By Doing Less

Remember, a content marketing department supply chain looks like this:

- You come up with an idea for a piece of content
- You write the content
- You edit the content
- You manage the writing and editing of the content
- You post the content
- You ask other people to post the content
- You pay other people to post, share, and backlink to the content
- You pay to boost / promote the content
- You manage the posting, and the sharing, and the back-linking of the content
- And then you count up how many views, Likes, comments, shares, backlinks, and (maybe) sales the content accumulated.

The massive opportunity we see here is to flip this pyramid.

Right now, the "idea" portion of the content marketing supply chain, the nucleus, the "thinking," has at most 10% priority. Most companies (and content marketing departments) over-invest in resources to edit, post, cross-post, promote, and manage the content and massively under-invest in, say, hiring a legendary journalist, ghostwriter, or world-class content creator to get the ball rolling in a DIFFERENT direction. In fact, we would argue that most large-scale companies would be 100x better off reducing the person-power of their content marketing departments by 50-90% and reallocating those resources to publishing higher quality, more differentiated content less often. (Not to break our own arms patting ourselves on the back, but Category Pirates is a perfect example of this. We do very little to outwardly promote rah-rah-look-at-us promote our newsletter, and in record time we've climbed the Substack charts. That's because we spend the vast majority of our time thinking about, debating, and refining what we're saying—not amplifying as many mediocre ideas as we can fit into a monthly "content calendar.")

Here's what this means for a variety of roles in the marketing world:

- **If you are a CEO or founder,** what is your differentiated insight? What problem are you solving? Why do you care (like all missionaries do) about your category, company, and products? Why should others care? What difference are you trying to make for others? Without giving yourself time to do some different thinking, you will not be fresh. It is so easy to get crushed in a traffic jam of Zooms that you can't even hear yourself think... nevermind *actually* think. The "E" in CEO is for Evangelist. And before you can start evangelizing, you need to know what you really think.

- **If you are a CMO,** this idea that you need to be proficient in as many different marketing platforms and disciplines as possible is nonsense. Again, these are all tactics—and as a CMO, your #1 job is strategy. It really doesn't matter if you understand how to run a Facebook ad or can set up a Mailchimp integration if the content and overarching POV you are going to plug *inside* those mechanisms is "The key to business is providing value to your customers." Instead, we encourage you to spend 99% of your time reading (mini-books like these!), thinking, questioning your thinking, debating your thinking with others, spending an insane amount of time with customers and coming to DIFFERENT conclusions, and then rejecting the accepted premise and asking why. Your job is to constantly scour your brain for breakthrough ideas hiding in plain sight that everyone else in your industry is missing.

- **If you are a marketing manager,** and you want to have a massive impact within your company, your path to getting there is not "more content, more often." It's actually to make the controversial decision to do the opposite: less content, less often, with more resources dedicated to getting your hands on truly differentiated thinking (and dismantling any red tape getting in your way of achieving this goal). Now, to be clear, we don't think writing 1 world-class blog post per year is the right strategy either (although it sure is better than "Hustle!" quote graphics). The content marketing supply chain you want to design is one that optimizes for the highest level of quality without compromising quantity, and vice versa. Volume is good— but only if it's quality volume.

- **If you are a content writer,** and you're tired of being paid $25 per blog post, the single fastest way to increase your value (and earnings) is to provide differentiated thinking. Content writers are treated as commodities because many think their job is to "write 800 words." Alrighty, here's a bunch of words: "Giraffes and a llama with a toaster business stuff is the key so don't you forget it and by the way eat Rice Krispies." Is any of that valuable? Of course not. Word count is a terrible measure of value. Which means if you are charging "per word" as a content writer, you are declaring to companies you are easily replaceable. (And now, GPT-3 technology can do what you do.) But if you start charging for your *thinking* and provide companies not just with words, but unique, unheard of, unidentified perspectives on the category, suddenly you are a luxury good. How much would a company pay for a unique and differentiated POV?

If you are a half-decent writer, mediocre marketer, but a courageous thinker, you can make a boatload (*ARRRRRRRR!!!!*) of money helping Content Marketing Industrial Complexes find their soul again.

(And from a business perspective, make the cash register sing again.) For example, Pirate Cole has built a legendary career working with startup founders, company executives, and investors on refining their thinking and publishing their unique insights at scale on the Internet (and there's a reason Pirate Cole is 100x+ more expensive than the "ghostwriters" you find on Upwork.com). But what's important to note here is it's not "marketing tricks" or "growth hacks" that makes this content stand out. It's the conversations being had that push the thinking into uncharted territory (as well some "therapy sessions" with the aspiring thought leaders encouraging them, "It's OK to be different").

Unfortunately, by the looks of the data, the content marketing world is an accelerating muscle car and the breaks have blown out.

Over the next few years, we are likely going to see more and more companies fall into the trap of "more content, more often." But rarely in life are we presented with such an obvious opportunity to be radically different. What's also radically clear is that most marketers will not do it. They will keep pumping out pablum—as they build out their ever-expanding content-free marketing industrial complex.

We think this is a multi-billion dollar opportunity for those willing to "think" different.

CHAPTER FOUR

The Art Of Fresh Thinking

How To Create Obvious & Non-Obvious Content

Which leads us to... how to think different!

What is "thinking?"

According to Roger Martin, arguably the world's #1 management thinker, "thinking" is when you look at the world through an existing model. It's how we use learnings from the past to make sense of the present—which is critical when you're, for example, driving down the highway. When another driver cuts you off, you instantly apply your past experiences to the present and swerve to avoid an accident. Your reflex saves your life.

But here's the rub: almost all thinking is what Roger calls "reflexive." Which means our mental scaffolding for thinking is *the past*.

Let's play a game:

Read the following words (slowly) and just notice what happens in your brain.

- Guns
- Abortion
- Flat earth
- Billionaires
- Democrats
- Republicans
- Free-speech
- Climate change

What did you notice?

Did you have any immediate reactions? Do you already have an opinion?

Almost all thinking is reflexive (having an unconscious "reflex" in response) versus what Roger calls "reflective" (taking a moment to consciously reflect on how the past may have created a preexisting mental model keeping you from considering a new and different future).

For example, someone says: "If you're not for the 1st amendment, then you're anti-American."

The recipient of this opinion experiences a reflex—like when a doctor slams a tiny pink hammer against your kneecap and your leg jolts upward—and they immediately say in response, "I'm not anti-American! You're anti-American for even thinking that about me!"

This exchange is more akin to the mental Retweeting of information we agree or disagree with—without any meaningful *reflection*.

Which causes a scarcity of fresh thinking in the world.

Actual "thinking" is not reflexive. It's reflective.

You are presented with information.

You become conscious of which model you are using to evaluate the information (which "lens" you are looking through).

And then *before* you react, respond, or give in to your reflexive nature, you pause and first consider which mental model you're using to examine the information being presented. You train yourself to be curious, to ask why, to suspend your past opinions, beliefs, and mental models, and to open the aperture of your mind and consider something different.

That's "thinking."

(Which is very different from what most people do, which is play a game of "I'm right, you're wrong" Ping-Pong—you talk, I talk; you talk, I talk—no one really listening or actually thinking.)

What most people call listening is actually called "waiting to talk."

The Art Of Strategic (Fresh) Thinking

With the above in mind, then "strategic thinking" (which is maybe one of the most overused yet misunderstood phrases in all of academia and business) is not what most people think it is.

The vast majority of conventional wisdom and strategy is thinking "what has been true" about the past.

- Harvard Business School students read ~500 case studies (about the past) during their 2 years of study.

Good to Great by Jim Collins is all about comparing similar companies (from the past).

McKinsey's own website says that strategy is based on the past:

> *"Creative data mining enables us to produce privileged insights and finely calibrate strategies that we know work; these are not simply theoretical claims backed by a few*

*cases but rather statistically valid ones based on large-sample learnings from nearly **100 years of experience**."*

The vast majority of content about strategic thinking comes from academia and strategy consulting firms. And thinking about "what has been true in the past" is deeply rooted in their DNA. When you hire (most) management consulting firms, what you're really buying is a detailed analysis of what worked *yesterday*. This is exactly what technology analyst firms like Gartner do. They explain the past.

Academia takes it one step further. Academics can't publish without extensive research about the past. And any new information has to be rigorously peer reviewed by other professors who are experts about the past. The pinnacle of being an economics or business school professor is winning the Nobel prize. But the Nobel prize in economics is typically awarded for work completed *decades ago* (based on analyses of data even before that)!

Neither of these are accurate (or effective) definitions of truly strategic thinking.

Strategy, in its purest form, is the art of the possible.

It's the process of considering "what could be true."

- What new mental model would have to be invented for this to work?
- What if people moved *from* the way it is, *to* a new and different way?
- What if a new outcome (an outcome we haven't considered before) was possible?

For example: in 2008, the idea of Airbnb made no sense when evaluated through old mental models. As a result, nearly every venture capitalist said, "No way. You can't rent out your living room as if it's a hotel. That's insane. Probably illegal. What if someone gets killed in

their sleep, or raped? And you really think people a 110
to share a kitchen, or a toilet, with someone they've n
Only a very small handful of investors (including the
Sequoia Capital) had the courage and mental awarenes
ent question—a "thinking" question: "What would need to be true for
this idea to work?" And what they ended up concluding was that the
idea of Airbnb didn't make sense when evaluated through previously
established mental models—but it *did* make sense through the lens of
a new model (a model that was not unfathomable). In fact, it was likely
a decade away from being completely acceptable—and thus, "worth the
risk" (which helped Sequoia turn roughly $280 million invested over
multiple rounds into more than $12 billion).

(Every legendary business is a dumb idea. Until it isn't.)

But these moments are rare. Most people (whether they realize it
or not) are trapped in backward-looking reflexive thinking. As a result,
their "strategic thinking" regresses into an exercise of *evaluating the
future against the past* (this is how management consultants put "food
on the family"). But there is no thoughtful, **reflective** discussion about
what "could" be true (the art of the possible). Only **reflexive** Ping-Pong
monologues about how hypotheses about the future do not make sense
against the mental models of yesterday.

Remember: everything is the way it is because somebody changed
the way it was.

Some of the "smartest" people on planet earth lose this thread. Some
of the smartest people stopped reflective thinking a long time ago. We
would even go so far as to say that being declared a smart person is almost
certain to make you stupid. Because when you get called "smart," you
become entrenched in your comfortable past. When you're smart, you
know things. And most people who know things are called "experts."
Which means they *already* know. And when you *already know,* by
definition you are using old mental scaffolding when considering new

...d different futures.

Which makes you stupid.

So, don't strive to become an expert (ever!).

Because being an expert is the enemy of fresh thinking.

In martial arts there is a manta called "white belt for life"... because fighting is like life. You'll either be humble in life, or humbled by it.

How To Create Obvious & Non-Obvious Content

In order to build the skill of coming up with fresh, new ideas, we have to first define what it means to "think."

And here's why:

- **Obvious Content** = The art of speaking to what people already think and believe (catering to the reader's *reflexive* nature).

- **Non-Obvious Content** = The art of educating people on what they haven't thought about or decided they believe yet (requesting their *reflective* nature).

It's crucial to understand which of these two consumption states you are creating for, and where you are "meeting the reader"—long before you write even a single word. Because if you try feeding Non-Obvious content (that requires reflection and a challenging of one's own mental models) to someone in an Obvious (reflexive) state, you will fail to get their attention and/or they'll likely become frustrated at your inability to cater to their preconceived notions. And conversely, if you try feeding Obvious content to someone starving for Non-Obvious insights, you will burden them with boredom and/or they'll likely become frustrated with your wasting their time, even insulting them ("This is so Obvious! Make me think!").

Reflexive readers want Obvious content.

Reflective readers want Non-Obvious content.

Knowing who you are creating for, and what their expectations are (and why) is half the battle to becoming a legendary writer, creator, and/ or entrepreneur.

The Obvious/Non-Obvious Spectrum

We Pirates are Non-Obvious thinkers, Category Designers, and writers—and are clearly biased in "thinking" in Non-Obvious ways.

However, we want to emphasize the importance of Obvious thinking. In fact, when you are a beginner (trying to learn anything), Obvious action steps and incremental insights are exactly what you need. If you are trying to learn how to play the piano and a world-class pianist sits down and starts explaining Non-Obvious ornamental variations, you will have no idea what to do with that information. Furthermore, you'll become frustrated. You'll feel as though the person you sought out for (Obvious) education wasn't meeting you where you are—triggering all your existing fears and further reinforcing your "newbie" nature.

Obvious and Non-Obvious thinking (and content) exists on a spectrum.

Both are meaningful and valuable to different types of consumers at different levels of learning. (There is a time and a place to play Chopin. And there is a time and place to play chopsticks.)

But as you'll soon discover, the art (and business) of becoming a legendary writer, creator, or entrepreneur is about finding strategic ways to move up and out of Obvious, incremental instruction and into exponential Non-Obvious thinking.

This is what puts you in a category of one.

And this is where you make the biggest difference.

Problem, Solution, Outcome

However, in order to "sell" the world on your ideas, you need to effectively communicate the value of each idea in a clear and concise manner.

All ideas have the same 3 components:

- Problem
- Solution
- Outcome

It doesn't matter if you write 6 words or 600 words or 6,000 words or 60,000 words. The reader or customer doesn't care how many words you write or how much effort you put into crafting the idea. All they care about is the problem you are solving, the solution you are providing, and the outcome you are unlocking for them. And to decide whether or not your "message" or idea (category) is worth their time, the reader/customer then weighs the perceived benefits of your problem, solution, and outcome against their own expectations.

- "If I believe this problem you're framing is real, then how bad has my life been with this unknown problem lingering for so long?"
- "If I use this solution, how much more effective will I be in solving this problem?"
- "If I unlock this outcome, how am I different? What will my life be like?"

Conventional wisdom here says that with this simple framework in mind, your job as a writer, creator, or entrepreneur is to figure out how to solve problems "better" than everyone else, or how to provide "better" solutions, or how to unlock "better" outcomes than the competition.

But this is reflexive thinking (which means it's a very bad strategy). Your job is not to look at other people's ideas, give in to an emotional reflex ("I'm going to crush you!!!"), and try to create something "better."

Your job is to reflect on your own mental models, "think," and introduce the world to ideas that are new, different, and fresh.

Here's exactly how to do that:

4 Stages Of Creation

As a writer or creator, what you really are is an "Intellectual Capitalist" whose job is to "think"—and then to find ways to leverage that thinking into net-new value.

There are 4 stages of creation:

- **Least Valuable:** Obvious, Obvious
- **More Valuable Near-Term:** Obvious, Non-Obvious
- **More Valuable Long-Term:** Non-Obvious, Obvious
- **Too Complicated:** Non-Obvious, Non-Obvious

On one side of the spectrum (Obvious, Obvious), the same thing that makes your "thinking" simple to understand and easily accepted is also what makes it undifferentiated and commoditized. You are just another writer, thinker, and creator saying the same things everyone else is—feeding the noisy narrative of the zeitgeist. (Think of the millions of hustleporn stars, for example.)

On the other side of the spectrum (Non-Obvious, Non-Obvious), your thinking is so out-of-the-box, so ahead of its time, that people struggle to wrap their minds around it. It's differentiated to an almost unusable degree. Which puts you in the camp of all the other writers, thinkers, and creators who believe themselves to be brilliant, but can't quite figure out how to get everyone else to see it too.

The secret is in the middle: to be Obvious in Non-Obvious ways, or to be Non-Obvious in Obvious ways.

The reason is because without both, your ideas are either so rudimentary (Obvious) they're commodities, or they're so complicated or unexpected (Non-Obvious) they're confusing—*which is just a different flavor of stupid.* And when people are confused, their reflexive brain tells them to dismiss the idea and just move on.

Which is why the most valuable ideas (meaning the ones that create the most net-new value for both the creator and the consumer) incorporate both.

So that you can add this new model to your own mental toolkit, let's walk through each one:

Obvious, Obvious

Obvious Problem
Obvious Solution
Obvious Outcome
Pun intended, but this is about as "obvious" as it gets.

Most writers (without even realizing it) spend their entire careers stuck on the Obvious, Obvious side of the spectrum. They write about things like "how to be more productive" or "how to ask for a raise at work" (Obvious problems), but then provide answers and share insights like "remove distractions" and "when asking for a raise, speak with confidence" (Obvious solutions) that help the reader unlock Obvious, already desirable goals like "I became slightly more productive" or "I got the 3% raise I wanted" (incremental Obvious outcomes). As a result, these writers, thinkers, and creators are a dime a dozen. Their content is so similar to what already exists, with "thinking" that is easily replaceable, that they spend their entire careers stuck in the "Better" trap—forever comparing themselves to the next Obvious, Obvious writer and trying to out-Obvious them.

Unfortunately, this is what gives many of these writers, thinkers, and creators The "Me" Disease, causing them to look for other more extravagant ways to attract attention. (Since their content is Obvious and undifferentiated, they need to find another way to differentiate themselves.)

Here's an Obvious, Obvious example:

[**Obvious Problem**]: I'm overweight but I don't know how to lose weight.

[**Obvious Solution**]: Eat less carbs and fatty foods. Exercise more.

[**Obvious Outcome**]: Lose 10 pounds in 3-6 months.

Notice how even reading this Obvious problem, Obvious solution, and Obvious outcome sort of puts you to sleep. In less than 20 words you feel like you've extracted all of the value from this "thinking." You have nothing more to gain—which means your attention is already in search of more "mental nutritional value" elsewhere. (Which is why the average tweet from a typical business "thought leader" is intellectual fast food.)

Now, before we introduce you to Non-Obvious thinking, some words of caution about the siren call of a niche within Obvious, called Obvious *Stupid*.

An entire generation of entrepreneurs, creators, and writers have been duped into thinking that spewing Obvious Stupid, everywhere, as often as possible, is the road to success. We wrote about this extensively in our mini-books, *Content-Free Marketing* and *The "Me" Disease*. In some ways, you can't blame them. Zillions of content-free Tweets, LinkedIn updates, and blog posts (like this one from real-estate entrepreneur Grant Cardone that says: "Big success does not come without big challenges.") litter the Internet. And many readers Like, and even Comment and contribute their own Obvious Stupid responses ("Big success also requires big risk!"). This happens because what most people call thinking *is not thinking*. It's reflexive Liking of Obvious Stupid ideas that make them feel comforted.

For a second.

Hustleporn stars and personal brand "influencers" drive vanity metrics pumping Obvious Stupid. But doing this is a neon sign you're radically undifferentiated. And you're making little difference and zero contribution to *actual thinking*. Worst of all, when you play this game, you have to spend massive amounts of money to spread massive amounts of Obvious Stupid. Because you're playing an attention game (like a child who incessantly begs for Mom's attention purely for the sake of it).

Now, let's say the quiet part out loud: everyone with an IQ larger than their shoe size knows this stuff is Obvious Stupid. But the reason it works is the same reason America has an obesity epidemic and can't stop eating sugar-filled processed foods: because, in the moment, it's comforting. When 692 other people Like an Obvious Stupid tweet, the 693rd person reflexively thinks, "If 692 other people Like this, maybe I should too." They are the true definition of a follower—wired to "fit in." It's the same reason why lemmings jump off cliffs into the ocean—because other lemmings are jumping. Hustleporn stars and "influencers" know this, which is why many of them pay to create the facade of "social proof," buy Likes, Followers, reviews, downloads, and even mass quantities of their own books. Because they know if they create the impression that the lemmings are leaping, the actual lemmings might leap.

The question we would encourage you to ask yourself is: what does your future look like if all your followers are interested in hearing about from you is Obvious Stupid? Is that really what you want?

(The answer is: your life becomes a hamster wheel of endlessly telling the lemmings which way is up.)

Obvious, Non-Obvious

- Obvious Problem
- Non-Obvious Solution
- Obvious Outcome

Obvious problems usually unlock Obvious outcomes.

Non-Obvious problems usually unlock Non-Obvious outcomes.

Think of them as barbells. The problem and the outcome mirror each other. And the solution is the bridge between them in the middle.

With this in mind, the easiest way to immediately differentiate yourself as a writer, thinker, and creator is to take an Obvious problem, solve it in a Non-Obvious way, and unlock an Obvious, already desirable outcome.

This is how Pirate Cole was able to successfully quit his 9-5 job in his mid-20s and build a ghostwriting firm for executives. The Obvious problem was that founders, CEOs, and investors wanted to share their thoughts and insights online. And a gazillion PR firms already solved that problem in Obvious ways: they would get these founders, CEOs, and investors quotes or bylines in major publications. But Pirate Cole had spent 3 years writing on Quora and discovered that not only did Quora provide 10x more distribution than every single major publication on the Internet, but Quora also had syndication partnerships with major publications—so certain Quora answers could also end up in *Forbes, Inc Magazine, Fortune, Business Insider*, etc. When founders and CEOs said to him, "I want to share my thoughts online" or "I want to be published in a major publication," Pirate Cole gave them a Non-Obvious solution. "Publish on Quora and your most popular pieces will likely end up in major publications, but you'll also get 10x more exposure because of the nature of Quora's social algorithms."

Obvious problem, Non-Obvious solution.

And this is how Pirate Cole built a multimillion-dollar ghostwriting agency working with hundreds of founders, executives, and investors in less than 18 months.

Here's another Obvious, Non-Obvious example:

[**Obvious Problem**]: I want to get into real estate so I have some passive revenue.

[**Non-Obvious Solution**]: Don't buy buildings and be a landlord. Keep your money, and instead rent an attractive apartment and charge a premium by renting it out again on Airbnb (while you crash on your buddy's couch).

[**Obvious Outcome**]: I have passive revenue without having to invest big money to get started.

Notice what makes you "different" here is the Non-Obvious solution you are providing as the bridge between the Obvious problem and

Obvious outcome. This is why so many writers use words like "secrets" in book titles and sales materials. "Secrets" implies Non-Obvious solutions to Obvious problems. The stress test, however, is whether the "secrets" you are sharing are truly Non-Obvious (and thus differentiated and valuable), or if you are trying to use a marketing word to make up for the fact that you are still solving an Obvious problem, and trying to unlock an Obvious outcome, using Obvious "already known" solutions.

Here's another Obvious, Non-Obvious example:

[**Obvious Problem**]: I want my kids to eat their veggies and I don't want to fight about it.

[**Non-Obvious Solution**]: Don't feed them plain broccoli. Melt a little bit of ooey-gooey-drooly Velveeta on top of it.

[**Obvious Outcome**]: Clean plates. Happy household.

Non-Obvious solutions to Obvious problems tend to lead people to smack their foreheads and say, "Melted cheese on broccoli? Why didn't I think of that?!"

Non-Obvious, Obvious

- Non-Obvious Problem
- Obvious Solution
- Non-Obvious Outcome

The most valuable part of the creation spectrum is when you can solve Non-Obvious problems in Obvious ways. This is the intellectual equivalent of MacGyver using an ordinary (Obvious) tool to solve a Non-Obvious problem, or Jason Bourne using a rolled-up newspaper to fight off an attacker with a knife.

The reason is because when someone already knows something is a problem, they have also determined the "value" of the solution. But when someone *does not know* something is a problem, and you come along and reveal to them how and why this problem is urgent and important, they are going to have a much harder time "valuing" the solution—because this is the first time they've ever seen, heard of, or considered the problem!

Which means you can educate them on its value (price).

The key, however, is making Non-Obvious problems seem easy, simple, and "Obvious" to solve for. As we'll get into in the next section, if you present a Non-Obvious solution to a Non-Obvious problem, the person on the other side of the table is going to have a hard time a) understanding the urgency and importance of the problem, and b) understanding the importance and the action steps of the solution.

But when you educate a reader or customer about a Non-Obvious problem, and then give them an easy, simple, highly actionable Obvious solution, all of a sudden... POOF! Their life is changed forever. They are now aware of a problem that didn't exist in their consciousness before, and the moment they decide they need a solution, there you are (which makes you seem like a gift from the heavens).

For example:

[Non-Obvious Problem]: Writer's block doesn't happen because you're a bad writer, or uninspired, or unmotivated. Writer's block happens when you lack frameworks and templates you can pull from over and over again.

[Obvious Solution]: Here are a bunch of easy-to-use writing templates.

[Non-Obvious Outcome]: When you use these templates, not only is writer's block gone forever, but the likelihood of you writing something viral online goes up 50%.

Or here's another example from the legendary coffee company, Keurig:

[Non-Obvious Problem]: Office coffee sucks even though it is free—because not everyone likes the same kind of coffee.

[Obvious Solution]: Here's a single-serve cup of coffee in a tiny K-Cup so you can choose the specific roast, blend, origin and flavor just the way you like it.

[**Non-Obvious Outcome**]: Employees are happier with the coffee and employers are psyched that their workforce is more productive because they are well caffeinated and do not have to leave to go to Starbucks.

And this, fellow pirates, is why JAB acquired Keurig for $14 billion dollars in 2015.

Solving Non-Obvious problems in Obvious ways is also how Pirate Christopher went from starting a business at 18 years old (after getting thrown out of school) to landing three Silicon Valley public company CMO gigs and retiring at age 38.

He was radically differentiated because he framed a Non-Obvious problem.

And that problem goes like this:

During Pirate Christopher's days as a public tech company CMO, he made sure the world understood that he was a different CMO. His Non-Obvious point-of-view was: "I don't solve the problem most marketing executives solve. I help create and dominate categories."

Christopher differentiated himself by re-framing the conversation with a Non-Obvious problem that stopped CEOs in their tracks. And he ultimately went from being one of thousands of "tech marketing people" to being a "Godfather of Category Design."

Here's how a typical conversation between Christopher and a CEO would go: "Look, CEO. If you're lucky, you will find a good CMO who keeps the trains running on time, fills the sales pipeline, drives revenue, builds your brand, and works well with customers and analysts. And if that's what you're looking for, you should go hire that person. And while I know how to do that stuff, that's not where I add value. *As you know,* in every company's life, particularly in the tech business, there's often an 18-to-24-month window where a very serious category battle goes down that decides who is going to dominate that emerging category. Well,

I have a black belt in that. I know how to design and dominate categories, and I know how to take existing categories and redesign them to tilt the market agenda to our advantage. That's my superpower."

When you have that type of conversation, you've moved someone's thinking *from* "we need to hire a CMO" *to* "Holy cow, Batman! We need to win the category battle!"

A more extreme example of how valuable solving Non-Obvious problems with Obvious solutions can be is the category design work we now do with companies as Category Pirates. Because the Non-Obvious problem most companies face (ranging from startups all the way up to the S&P 500) is they don't have clarity over their unique and differentiated category. Further, they lack the languaging to successfully Name & Claim new territory in the customer's mind. When these founders, executives, or investors read Category Pirates and become aware of this Non-Obvious problem they didn't know they had, they reach out to us in search of an Obvious solution. (The Obvious solution being: hire us.)

Non-Obvious, Non-Obvious

- Non-Obvious Problem
- Non-Obvious Solution
- Non-Obvious Outcome

This is where the wheels fall off the whisky wagon.

Or, as Pirate Christopher loves to say, "Let's not be so smart we're stupid."

There is a tipping point where too much Non-Obvious thinking goes from being eye-opening to head-hurting. The reader or customer doesn't have enough "Obvious" to ground themselves. They need to "think about it." (Which really means they are dismissing the Non-Obvious.) People (generally) do not say to themselves, "Hmm, I have no idea about that. Cool. Let me dig into it."

And look: your Non-Obvious problem and Non-Obvious solution

might be interesting, or sound innovative and smart, but because there are no actionable next steps (nothing "Obvious" for the reader to hold onto), the conversation just sort of ends with a shrug.

For example:

[**Non-Obvious Problem**]: People don't have trouble sleeping because of the firmness of their mattress. They have trouble sleeping because of the temperature of their bed.

[**Non-Obvious Solution**]: You'll sleep better if the temperature of your bed is colder. To do this, you'll want to buy 12 ice packs and keep them at the foot of your bed underneath your covers.

[**Non-Obvious Outcome**]: While you are sleeping, if you let your toes rest against the tops of the ice packs, then you will not only sleep better but you will reduce the wrinkling of the skin underneath your feet.

Now, reading the above, we'd bet your inner monologue is saying, "OK so obviously I'm not going to do any of that." Neither would we. But it's important to consider why. And the reason is because it's very difficult to see the clear, actionable link between Non-Obvious problems and Non-Obvious solutions. In order for you to wrap your mind around it, one of them has to be Obvious. Either the problem has to be known but the viable solution unknown, or the problem has to be unknown but the viable solution made known.

But having neither is sort of like being asked to solve for X when you also don't know what the other variables in the equation mean.

That said, triple Non-Obvious scenarios can work and be successful—but it can be difficult to realize their full potential.

Consider American Girl:

[**Non-Obvious Problem**]: Little girls want to play with dolls. Moms, aunts, and grandmothers have fond memories of playing with Barbies—but wanted a toy that was more educational and aspirational.

[**Non-Obvious Solution**]: Create dolls based on historical fictional characters. Price them 10x more than Barbies. Create books, films, and a retail experience (a la Disneyland) in the most expensive real estate in key cities where little girls can bring their $100 dolls to have tea and make matching pajamas along with Mom, Auntie, and Grandma.

[Non-Obvious Outcome]: Little girls will have a blast playing, but also read more, be better educated, and feel more empowered, all while Mom, Auntie and Grandma have a great time with just the girls.

Pirate Eddie has two daughters, and wrote about American Girl in his book *Superconsumers*—and yet American Girl still remains "Non-Obvious" for him!

American Girl is an amazing business, but has had trouble scaling beyond a few hundred million dollars in revenue. And even though Mattel acquired it in 1998 to have in its portfolio along with Barbie, Mattel has not figured out how to tap into its magic to grow either American Girl, Barbie, or its entire business. It is now in discussions with private equity to go private. (Non-Obvious is hard!)

A little more "Obvious" may have helped American Girl grow. It also may have helped Mattel figure out if there was a way to apply its business model to its Hot Wheels franchise. Or perhaps sell American Girl to Disney, who is the Category King of solving triple Non-Obvious scenarios and businesses.

The Languaging Effect

Incorporating languaging across this spectrum is where things get interesting.

(A demarcation point in language, creates a demarcation point in thinking, which creates a demarcation point in actions and results.)

At each stage of creation—Obvious, Obvious / Obvious, Non-Obvious / Non-Obvious, Obvious / Non-Obvious, Non-Obvious—there is an opportunity to find a new way to "language" the problem, the solution, and/or the outcome.

After all, **you can't talk about new things with old language.**

For example, notice the difference between the framing of these two Obvious problems:

1. "You are struggling with comparing yourself to others."
2. "You are struggling with Writer's Envy."

Which one are you drawn to more? Which one do you feel more emotionally connected to? Which one do you think you'll remember 5-10 minutes from now? The answer is you'll remember the second one because it uses languaging: the strategic use of language to change thinking. Languaging is when you Name & Claim an idea by calling it something—and in some cases draw further attention to it by capitalizing the term as if it exists on its own. (You might read that second example and then Google the term "Writer's Envy." The fact the words are capitalized leads your brain to believe it's "a thing.")

When we name an idea as something unique, it gains in power. (What's the difference between livestock and pets? *Names.*) Languaging is so incredibly powerful, and so underutilized, even by some of the most talented writers in the world, that regardless of what type of content you are creating (Obvious or Non-Obvious), languaging can oftentimes be the X factor that separates you from everyone else.

Here's a quick crash course:

- **Languaging to niche down:** The founder of Gumroad, Sahil Lavingia, wrote a book called *The Minimalist Entrepreneur.* Most people would read this title and think, "Hey, that's pretty clever!" But beneath the hood, what's really happening is Sahil is differentiating between entrepreneurs who build companies with lots of venture capital (he should have Named & Claimed those too—maybe something like Maximalist Entrepreneurs!) and entrepreneurs who bootstrap companies themselves with very little funding or startup resources (Minimalist

Entrepreneurs). As a result, "Minimalist Entrepreneurship" is now a niche inside the broader Entrepreneurship category. And so if you want to learn about entrepreneurship in general, this probably isn't the book for you. But if you want to learn about Minimalist Entrepreneurship, and how to bootstrap a company, then this book is exactly for you.

- **Languaging to Name & Claim an idea:** The best-selling book, *The Tipping Point*, is maybe the greatest example of how powerful languaging can be to differentiate an already existing idea. *The Tipping Point* basically means "the moment at which word-of-mouth marketing goes massively viral." This wasn't a new idea. There are over 5,000 books on Amazon about "word of mouth marketing." But Malcolm Gladwell was the first person to use languaging and call that moment something. This is the power of languaging, and it can be used to Name & Claim existing ideas that haven't been properly "packaged" (or called something) yet—or can be used to Name & Claim net-new ideas.

- **Languaging to invent a new term:** Little insider secret here, but we (along with a handful of other legendary pirates) invented the words "Category Design." 10 years ago, those two words next to each other didn't exist. We invented the term, defined it, and then evangelized and built an industry around it. Today? People put in their job descriptions, "I am a Category Designer." And CEOs ask headhunters to find them a "Category Designer." Because Category Design is now a thing (a category). And a very valuable thing at that. *Arrrrrrrr!!!!!!*

(As a side note, if you consider us teachers, then we are among the

*few teachers who practice what we teach. All day. Every day. Because
to create the category of Category Design, we have to practice Category
Design and teach it—at the same time.)*

Most writers go their entire careers never realizing that the big secret
to being seen as a brilliant thinker and writer tends to come down to languaging. Languaging creates different futures. (O.J. Simpson was found
not guilty in the murder of Nicole Simpson and Ron Goldman because
of powerful languaging. "If the glove doesn't fit, you must acquit.") We
remember ideas that are packaged nicely and given a name much more
easily than we remember them in sentences of explanation.

Notice the name of this section you're reading: The Languaging
Effect.

We are using languaging to Name & Claim the term "languaging,"
as well as the effect languaging can have on your writing—using languaging to teach languaging!

How To Generate Non-Obvious Ideas

There is a lot of Obvious content in the world about how to create
Obvious ideas. Anything "how to A to B" is Obvious.

The short answer for how to make Obvious content seem Non-
Obvious is by using languaging to niche down, Name & Claim an idea,
and/or invent a new term. (It's not word-of-mouth marketing. It's *The
Tipping Point*! It's not "hire a cleaning service and a dog walker so you
spend less time doing things you don't enjoy and can easily outsource."
It's *4-Hour Work Week!*).

The real question is how to come up with Non-Obvious ideas.

- How do you spot Non-Obvious problems?
- How do you create Non-Obvious solutions?
- How do you unlock Non-Obvious outcomes?

The challenge here is that when you are trying to come up with Non-Obvious insights, what you are really doing is solving an equation with no known/understood variables. This is the higher math of thinking and language. Furthermore, Non-Obvious insights tend to happen at the intersection of two or more conflicting data points or perspectives. That's what makes them Non-Obvious. Which means you need to train your mind to hold opposing, seemingly unrelated ideas long enough for your mental model (as we talked about at the beginning) to consider, "What must be true?"

Ah, but we sort of just gave you a Non-Obvious solution to a Non-Obvious problem, now didn't we!

Let us give you a more Obvious (and actionable) solution to the Non-Obvious problem called, "How do I generate Non-Obvious ideas?"

Today's solutions are tomorrow's problems.

Pirate Christopher remembers in the late 1970s and early 1980s when laser printers were invented.

It was a tremendous invention (created by Gary Starkweather), and unlocked all sorts of benefits for users—producing high-quality text and graphics, in color, using a laser. It was arguably the most innovative product to come out of Xerox, and created a massive category known as Digital Printing.

But laser printers had a downside: cartridges were expensive. So this innovative solution (the laser printer) created a new problem called: laser printer cartridge replacement. Which meant, all of a sudden, small businesses and 3rd party sellers started popping up everywhere—offering to refill cartridges for a fraction of the cost to replace them (an Obvious solution).

Which then created a new problem: people would pay for their cartridges to get refilled, and then not know how to replace them inside their laser printers. Which led to the creation of a new solution: laser cartridge replacement services. And so on and so on: a solution creating a problem, creating a new solution, creating a new problem.

This is the evolution of society in a nutshell.

(One day, might we have so many robots dealing with so many new and different problems in our house that we'll need a mega-super-duper-ding-dong robot to manage all the minion robots?)

In order to spot, create, or unlock Non-Obvious problems, solutions, or outcomes, here's the easiest place to start:

Audit today's newest, hottest, most popular solutions.

Solutions create problems, and problems create categories.

By auditing the solutions society values most heavily *today*, what you're going to find are emerging categories with strong tailwinds behind them. This means today's solutions are going to create tomorrow's problems, and solving tomorrow's problems before anyone else is just another way of saying "solving Non-Obvious problems."

These problems are Non-Obvious because the world hasn't realized which way the wind is blowing yet!

For example, cryptocurrencies are today's hot solution to an age-old problem called "banks and other 3rd parties get in the way of my money." But today's solutions create tomorrow's problems, and as soon as you buy your first Bitcoin, all of a sudden you are confronted by a slew of new and different problems: how do you safely store the seed phrase to your crypto wallet? Do you even have a cold storage wallet? How do you buy your first cold storage wallet? How do you transfer cryptocurrencies between wallets? How do you protect yourself from getting hacked? Entrepreneurs, creators, and digital writers today are racing to solve these problems (with products, services, and education).

And when they do, those solutions will present new problems to be solved—and so on, and so on.

So, to recap:

- What are the solutions most highly valued by society today?
- What problems do those solutions create?
- And how can you be the first (or close to the first) to solve those emerging problems?

Don't catch waves. Create them.

There's a nuance in what we are saying—and we want to be explicit about it.

What you are NOT doing is trying to "catch" a new wave or trend. In the Obvious world, this is what reflexive thinkers "think" is innovation: something popular happens, and your job is to see and create a new solution *for the existing problem*.

That's not what we're saying.

If something becomes popular, or a new category emerges (meaning it has become Obvious), and if all you do is create an Obvious solution to that existing, emerging problem, then what you are really doing is "catching" (fighting for) demand. And while you can make a few bucks in the short term doing this, we are advocating for you to *think* one step further. **We want you to create demand.** Instead of having a reflexive reaction to today's innovations, reflect for a bit and think, "What could be true?" Consider what new, Non-Obvious problems today's solutions might create in the future—and go create them. Because not only will you be the first (or one of the first), but because you're the one pointing out the next new Non-Obvious problem, you can set the price and teach the market how (and how much) to value your solution.

This is where all exponential value is created.

For example (and we love this story because it's both literal and figurative), Kelly Slater, the greatest professional surfer of all time is also the founder of Kelly Slater Wave Co. It's a company that uses technology and a human-made wave pool to create "the perfect wave." This is an extremely meta example of how a Non-Obvious champion in surfing took his Non-Obvious creativity and applied it to (shall we language this?) Oceanic Entrepreneurship.

Kelly Slater, the ultimate Superconsumer of surfing, woke up one day and said, "I have a problem. And that problem is called: how do I surf the perfect wave, forever?" For every surfing Superconsumer, this problem is fairly Obvious. There isn't a surfer on planet earth who isn't sitting on a surfboard somewhere in search of "the perfect wave." But the Obvious solution to that problem has always been to go out and find the perfect wave (maybe it's in Indonesia?).

The Non-Obvious solution was to use technology and a giant wave pool to create that perfect wave, forever.

This is what we are advocating for—figuratively, but also literally.

The world's most exponential thinkers do not "catch" waves of popularity.

hey create them (by auditing today's solutions and preemptively solving tomorrow's problems).

How To Build Your Pirate Ship: The 5 Archetypes Of Highly Effective Creators

There are 5 archetypes for people who create Non-Obvious ideas in the world.

- **You are a Superconsumer:** You are passionate about something, and so you understand your own problems better than anyone else.
- **You are a Category Designer:** You can frame solutions to problems people didn't know they had.
- **You are a Languager:** You can use language to transform

a rational problem into an emotional one by "calling" it something.

- **You are a Visionary:** You can visualize Non-Obvious outcomes few people believe are possible.
- **You are a Missionary:** You are already living in the future, and will excitedly knock on people's doors in an effort to "spread the good word."

Each one of these archetypes has the potential to come up with Non-Obvious insights—all from different vantage points. And it's very possible that you are a magical combination of any or all of the above—a pirate wearing multiple pirate hats!

But exponential opportunities reveal themselves much more easily when two or more of these archetypes begin spending time with each other. (That's how the three of us decided to create Category Pirates.) When a Superconsumer and a Category Designer team up, or when a Visionary and a Languager team up? Watch out. And when all five get together? Game over. All three of us pirates learn a tremendous amount from each other, and (every single week) are in awe at the multiplier effect our friendship and collaboration has on each of us individually.

Here's a quick case-in-point example:

Most writers write by themselves. Writing tends to be thought of as a solo craft—and on the rare occasion that two or more people come together to write a byline or book, it's radically infrequent for that group of individuals to pen more than one or two works together. Very few duos become true partnerships. (Can you name a single group of two or more writers who came together for an extended period of time to create a legendary body of work? Ries and Trout, authors of *The 22 Immutable Laws of Marketing,* had a run. Any others?)

Category Pirates is a true trio. A "writing band." And the way we write is exactly the same way bands write and record. We even call it "jamming," and are inspired by bands like Metallica, The Rolling Stones,

U2, and Foo Fighters who've held together for decades on a shared mission. Each week, we hop on Zoom for 1-3 hours and talk. Sometimes, we walk in with an idea already rumbling around in one of our heads. Other times, an idea presents itself out of nowhere and we excitedly chase after it like a bunch of kids running after a rolling dodgeball across a playground. Who writes Category Pirates? We all do. Who comes up with the ideas? Sometimes Pirate Christopher, sometimes Pirate Eddie, and sometimes Pirate Cole. But when the idea comes out of the oven and the body of work is sitting on a dinner plate, none of us know (or can accurately remember) whose idea it was. Because it doesn't matter. We're a band. And so each of us identifies everything we create as "our own" and "the group's own," simultaneously. Our sense of connectedness and ownership for the work feels both personal and shared.

As a result, we are able to produce high-quality Non-Obvious content at a rate that would be impossible for one person.

Each of us, individually, was already a successful pirate.

But together, we have a pirate ship.

1 + 1 + 1 = 30 trillion.

As a writer, creator, and thinker, one of your top priorities in life should be to surround yourself with other pirates and build a pirate ship of your own. Because Supers tend to hang out with other Supers, and Languagers tend to hang out with other Languagers, and Visionaries tend to hang out with other Visionaries, and so on. And while spending time with other people "like you" may make you better in Obvious ways, it deprives you of all the Non-Obvious growth opportunities, ideas, and insights sitting at unlikely intersections.

Let's break down each archetype individually:

Pirate #1: Superconsumers

If you are still struggling to spot Non-Obvious problems worth solving, the easiest and most actionable way to gather ideas is to talk to the

Superconsumers of your industry.

These people will educate you about problems you didn't know you had. And they will use language that is far more emotional and aspirational than any CMO could ever imagine.

That's because when you are a Superconsumer of something, you're obsessed with it. You live it every day. You talk about it constantly. Your friends are Supers. You go to events and hang out with other Supers. You consume content about it. You consume content about the content. You spend all day, every day, thinking about this "thing" you love so much—and deep down, some part of you wishes more people existed in the world who would be willing to "nerd out" about it with you.

If you ask a Super what problems they are currently facing related to whatever their passion is, more times than not you'll trigger a 45 minute monologue on all the great disservices happening in their sliver of the universe. So much so, that your reaction (unless you are a Super of that "thing" yourself) will likely be, "Wow, this person is weird." But they're not weird. They are insanely knowledgeable about something niche, specific, and likely full of untapped value. Which means your job is to listen, "think," and consider what "must" be true.

But Supers can also be the ones to come up with Non-Obvious ideas themselves.

If you've ever watched Shark Tank, then you know this is the origin story for the vast majority of small business owners who go on the show. *"I have been mowing lawns for 20 years, and then one day I threw my back out emptying the lawn mower bag full of grass clippings. So I started thinking, 'How am I going to keep mowing lawns if I can't bend down to empty the lawn mower bag?' And that's how I created Lawn Autobag, the automatic bag emptying device for lawn mowers."*

When you are a Super of something, you are keenly aware of the unsolved problems (that you and others would be willing to pay a massive premium for) in your industry.

Pirate #2: Category Designer

Category Designers are trained to identify Non-Obvious problems. When a Superconsumer and a Category Designer team up, suddenly the Non-Obvious becomes Obvious (to them). The Category Designer is terrific at recognizing (and "listening for") Non-Obvious problems. And the Superconsumer is terrific at leveraging their domain expertise to be able to articulate and share Non-Obvious problems. So when the Category Designer hears a Non-Obvious problem spoken aloud, a little siren goes off in their head alerting them: Category opportunity! Category Opportunity!

And remember:

- When solving an Obvious problem, present a Non-Obvious solution.
- And when solving a Non-Obvious problem, present an Obvious solution.

But in order for readers/customers to care enough to solve this Non-Obvious problem, they need to be educated about why it matters.

Which is where Languagers thrive.

Pirate #3: Languager

Journalists, speechwriters, even lawyers tend to be terrific Languagers.

They have mastered the fundamentals of the written word, and possess an incredible awareness for the ways in which words trigger different thoughts and emotions in readers. The most legendary Languagers then take it upon themselves to coin new terms, Name & Claim ideas, and change definitions of stigmatized vocabulary—or, even better, invent different words with new and different meanings.

The problem Languagers tend to have, however, is a lack of visibility into Non-Obvious problems worth solving.

Being a proficient Languager is a bit like being a trained sniper without a target. Languagers have one of the most powerful skills on planet earth (the ability to strategically use language to change people's thinking), and yet even the most talented writers struggle to apply their talents in a direction of exponential potential. (It's no surprise that many brilliant writers spend their entire careers earning a fraction of what software engineers make, even though their skill sets are arguably just as scalable and valuable in a digital world of frictionless information.)

So, what's a Languager to do?

- Find a Superconsumer to educate you on a valuable, Non-Obvious problem you didn't know existed.
3. And find a Category Designer to help frame the importance of solving that problem (to get you fired up about Naming & Claiming it something people can't help but remember!).

The role of the Languager is to help communicate this Non-Obvious problem in such a way where the average person goes: "Woah! I never thought of it like that!"

The Languager can use strategic language to make the Non-Obvious seem Obvious (and therefore easy to understand and memorable).

Pirate #4: Visionary

But pinpointing a Non-Obvious problem, and creating an Obvious solution (or vice versa), isn't the end of the road.

The last leg of the journey requires you to find a Visionary who can help you imagine what the future will look like once this Non-Obvious problem is solved. This is the Elon Musk archetype, painting an outcome so Non-Obvious, so "out of this world," that even the most educated Superconsumer will say to themselves, "Wow, I didn't even know that was possible." (Elon Musk didn't say, "We're going to the moon!" He said, "Listen. Plan A is to go electric and save planet earth. If that doesn't work, Plan B is to hop aboard this rocket and go to Mars. And not to visit. To live.")

Visionaries live in the clouds—for good and bad. They can imagine Non-Obvious outcomes better than anyone, but have trouble keeping their feet on the ground long enough to turn their daydreams into reality. Which is why the effectiveness of a Visionary is multiplied when she or he is surrounded by other more grounded pirates.

Pirate #5: Missionary

Missionaries are Superconsumers already living in the future—who then travel back to the present to rescue more Supers.

That neighbor who bought a Tesla back in 2012? Missionary.

That family friend who started composting their food waste long before it was trendy and cool? Missionary.

If you've ever seen *The Matrix*, Neo is the Superconsumer. Morpheous is the Missionary.

The secret power of a Missionary is their ability to "get" the solution to a Non-Obvious problem before anyone else. As a result, they are the ones Superconsumers look to become friends with—because they are the easiest to educate. Once the Missionary "gets" the cool factor of a solution to a Non-Obvious problem, they tell everyone they can about it. And they are the most credible because they've "been there, done that."

But, sort of like a religious follower going door to door selling bibles, a Missionary might be ecstatic about the solution (the bible), but is going to need some help understanding the problem, first.

Where Is Your Pirate Ship Stuck?

Each creator archetype has its pros and cons.

Which means your job is to "reflect" (THINK!) on where your pirate ship is stuck, and decide who you need to bring aboard in order to productively advance forward on your mission and journey.

- If you are stuck in Obvious land and having a hard time finding Non-Obvious problems worth solving, go find yourself a Superconsumer.

- If you have a Non-Obvious problem, but aren't sure how to frame the solution in an urgent and important way for readers/customers, find a Category Designer.

- If you have a Non-Obvious problem that is framed well, but are still struggling for the solution to "click" and become super Obvious for readers/customers, find a Languager.

- If you have a languaged Non-Obvious problem and an Obvious solution, but haven't figured out how to paint an exponential, highly desirable Non-Obvious outcome, find a Visionary.

- And if you have all the above but need help knocking on doors and evangelizing your mission in the world, find a squad of Missionaries.

This is how you build your pirate ship.

CHAPTER FIVE

The Power Of A Point Of View

Everything Is The Way It Is Because Someone Changed The Way It Was

Thinking about thinking is the most important kind of thinking.

90% of what we've been taught about entrepreneurship, business strategy, and marketing is wrong.

When we say things like this, we are not trying to be provocative for provocative's sake.

The core issue is that 100% of what we've been taught is based on the past and doesn't reflect a future where many things might change. Every generation looks and laughs at prior generations and wonders, "How did those prior generations believe that? Look at what we didn't know!"

Well, why would we assume future generations wouldn't look at us the same way?

Our job as pirates is to help smart people like you understand the context of what it is you're looking at and thinking about. And in the world of business, entrepreneurship, and marketing, the vast majority of the conversation (and the advice that gets given as a result) makes one very simple, unconscious, unquestioned, under-discussed mistake:

It assumes the market.

Entrepreneurship advice like, "You want to find product-market fit," and other business strategies rooted in conventional wisdom start with the way "it is." For example, "disruption" is tied to "the way it is." Digital transformation is rooted in "the way it is." When a company announces on their quarterly earnings call, "We are going to disrupt the manufacturing industry," what they are really saying (which we would name as their Point Of View) is, "We see and accept the way the world is, and we are going to *change the way it currently is* to a better version of the way it currently is."

Now, because what we're talking about here is particularly nuanced, let us illustrate what we mean by drawing an analogy (pun intended, *Arrrrrr!*).

Van Gogh vs Picasso

The beginning of Picasso's career was spent, to put it bluntly, in Vincent Van Gogh's shadow.

Van Gogh and other Renaissance Impressionist artists had cultivated a style the world loved. This 19th-century art movement was composed of *"relatively small, thin, yet visible brush strokes, open composition, emphasis on accurate depiction of light in its changing qualities, ordinary subject matter, inclusion of movement as a crucial element of human perception and experience, and unusual visual angles.*" Impressionism was all about capturing the essence of the moment—particularly in terms of time and movement. Some of the most famous impressionist paintings are Claude Monet's "Haystacks," followed by Van Gogh's "The Wheat Field Behind St. Paul's Hospital, St. Rémy," both of which aimed to capture the movement of nature (in the form of textures, colors, and shading). And while Van Gogh's style certainly seemed "different," side by side, it still abided by many of the rules established in impressionism.

In an analogy, this is how most writers, creators, and entrepreneurs think about product creation, innovation, digital transformation, and marketing. They start with "what exists," and then aim to "disrupt" or "change" or "transform" **the way it is.** *They assume the market.* They say, "Impressionism is what people clearly want. So let's do impressionism, but *better.*"

And for 20 years, this is what Picasso did too.

He studied the greats. He learned from the impressionist artists who came before him. And, using the same set of rules, he composed beautiful works of art that were "better," but still very much rooted in the past. Put Picasso's early work beside Van Gogh's, and you would lump them into the same "category."

"*Thin, visible brush strokes, ordinary subject matter, inclusion of movement as a crucial element of human perception and experience, unusual visual angles,*" Picasso was still playing by the rules **someone else wrote.** He might have been executing the rules a bit differently, or with his own "style," but when the painting was hung to dry, it was still, by every definition, an "impressionist" (category) painting.

Then, in 1907, a little more than a decade into his career, Picasso began experimenting with a new style of painting.

He and another artist friend called it Analytical Cubism.

Cubism was defined as *"simple geometric shapes, interlocking planes, and later, collage,"* and predominantly went against the previous definitions of what "beautiful paintings" were supposed to look and feel like. So much so, the earliest Cubism paintings were hidden from the public. When Picasso finished his first large cubism composition, "Les Demoiselles d'Avignon," he chose to keep it out of sight for years—fearful the unconventional, angular images of women (tackling unconventional subject matter: prostitutes) would spark controversy.

Today, that painting is valued to be worth $1.2 billion, and (apparently) wins the "If you could only own 1 painting" game among billionaires.

Assuming the market isn't what made Picasso, Picasso.

Had Picasso continued down the path of Van Gogh, he would have become "a better Van Gogh," or maybe even "a different Van Gogh." He'd be considered a great impressionist artist, but one of many: Monet, Manet, Degas, Cézanne, Renoir, and so on.

Instead, the reason Picasso is one of the most well-known and highly valued artists of all time is because he stopped trying to create the future while simultaneously remaining rooted in the past. Said differently, he "quit" the game of Impressionism and he "created" a new game called Cubism.

Cubism is not "a better type of Impressionism."

Cubism is not "Impressionism transformed."

Cubism is not "Impressionism+."

Cubism is not "Impressionism 2.0."

Picasso taught the world that Impressionism and Cubism are two completely *different* things.

They are not comparable.

More importantly, what allowed Picasso to create a new category of art wasn't just that he called it something different (although the languaging "Cubism" certainly helped it stick). It was that he also changed the way he defined success—that is to say, he introduced a new Point Of View of what he believed a painting should be.

- **Impressionist Point Of View:** Thin, visible brush strokes; ordinary subject matter; inclusion of movement as a crucial element of human perception and experience; etc.

- **Cubism Point Of View:** Instead of depicting objects from a single viewpoint, the artist depicts the subject from a multitude of viewpoints to represent the subject in a greater context. Objects are analyzed, broken up, and reassembled to an abstracted form.

This new POV is what allowed Picasso to break and take *new* ground—and as a result, allowed customers to understand how and why Picasso was doing what he was doing.

Your POV is the script customers use in word-of-mouth marketing.

This is what we mean when we say 90% of what the world gets taught about entrepreneurship, business strategy, marketing, and any act of *creation* is wrong.

When a company says, "We are going to digitally transform the media industry," what they are really saying (listen to the words) is, "We are going to take **what exists** and make it digital." *Something exists. Then this new thing came along. And we're going to apply the new thing to the old thing, and call the old thing new.*

They start with the way it is, and aim to make the way it is "better" or "incrementally different."

They are Picasso at age 21, trying to be an impressionist painter like Vincent Van Gogh, but better.

This starting point (insignificant and nuanced as it may seem) is what then dictates every single outcome that unfolds. If your POV is bound to the way it already is, then you have just signed yourself up for a lifetime of competition (Picasso vs Van Gogh vs Monet vs Manet vs Renoir, etc.) before your journey has even started. Because when you start with *the way it is* (Impressionism), rather than the way it could be (Cubism), you constrain yourself from the start—and you don't even know it.

And some of the smartest, most brilliant writers, creators, and entrepreneurs do this every single day.

- "I am going to write the greatest personal development book ever written" = "I accept the personal development genre **as it currently exists,** and I am going to change the personal development genre based on the already established definition of what the personal development genre is."

- "I am going to create the greatest story you've ever seen" = "I accept the definition of what a story **as it currently exists,** and I am going to incrementally change what that story looks like based on the already established definition of what a story is supposed to be."

- "I am going to digitize the movie rental industry" = "I accept the movie rental industry **as it currently exists,** and I am going to incrementally change the movie rental industry based on the already established definition of what the movie rental industry is."

Writers, creators, founders, investors, bankers, lawyers, the vast majority of the business ecosystem takes whatever is placed in front of them and says, "I accept the premise." And there is very little questioning around whether we are having the right conversation (context) to begin with. As a result, a company or creator's POV is unconsciously established ("We are going to incrementally change the future **based on the past**"), and every product, document, and decision that unfolds from there follows that POV—resulting in a lifetime of comparison.

But you can't create a different future when your starting reference point is the past.

Here's an example.

In 2021, enterprise software company, Couchbase, said in it's S-1 IPO filing:

> "Our mission is to empower enterprises to build, manage and operate modern mission-critical applications at the highest scale and performance. Couchbase provides a leading modern database for enterprise applications. Enterprises rely on Couchbase to power the core applications their businesses depend on, for which there is no tolerance for disruption or downtime."

Now, look closely.

There is zero "different" in those words.

You could change the name of the company on the document to AWS, Oracle, SAP, MongoDB, Cloudera, and countless others in the database category, and you wouldn't be able to tell the difference.

They further write:

> "Our database is versatile and works in multiple configurations, from cloud to multi- or hybrid-cloud to on-premise environments to the edge, and can be run by the customer or managed by us. We have architected our database on the next-generation flexibility of NoSQL, embodying a "not only SQL" approach. We combine the schema flexibility unavailable with legacy databases with the power and familiarity of the SQL query language, the lingua franca of database programming, into a single, unified platform. Our cloud-native platform provides a powerful modern

database that serves the needs of both enterprise archi-
tects and application developers."

More zero "different."

Nothing in the language and the Point Of View suggests anything other than, "Here at Couchbase, we provide the same stuff as countless other companies in the database space. We take the past, and we make the past *better/faster/cheaper/smarter*, just like everyone else."

But let us never forget: there are zero cover bands in the Rock & Roll Hall of Fame.

Which is why we say (and will continue to say):

Thinking about thinking is the most important kind of thinking.

And thinking about the context is the most important way to start thinking.

Do you accept the premise?

If you live on the west coast (or have ever taken a vacation to California), then you've probably seen pelicans flying around in the sky. These pelicans hunt fish from above, wait for the perfect moment to strike, and then "dive bomb" down into the water and emerge with a fish in their gullets.

If you are one of those fish, you spend your entire life living in water. All you know, and all you've ever seen, is water. You "accept the premise." From the moment you were born, water. Your fish parents, all they ever talk about is water. Your aunts and uncles, brothers and sisters, all live happily ever after in water. Not once, ever, do you question whether or not you live in water. Everywhere you see is water. Why would there be anything except water?

Until one day, a pelican swoops down, and scoops you up out of the ocean.

And in the final two seconds of your life, you realize water isn't the only thing that exists.

And then you're dead.

This is exactly what happens to companies & creators that "accept the premise."

One day, you're the largest "movie rental" retailer in the United States (Blockbuster).

And the next, all the oxygen has been sucked out of the room and you're irrelevant (Netflix—whoops).

For example, if you've spent your entire career working in manufacturing, "manufacturing" is your water. All you know is manufacturing. Your dad worked in manufacturing, and so did your dad's dad. You studied manufacturing in college. Your first internship was at a manufacturing facility. And for thirty years, all you've done and all you've ever known was steel and supply chains and good o'l fashioned manufacturing. You "accept the premise."

Until one day, somebody comes along with a different POV.

They change the premise—suddenly, manufacturing doesn't matter anymore—and render your job, your career, and your entire way of life irrelevant.

POVs move the world from the way it is to a new, different way.

Everything is the way it is because somebody changed the way it was.

Why were hotels suing Airbnb when the startup first started gaining traction? Why was Airbnb being labeled as an "illegal hotel?" (Notice how the angry hotels had to use old language to drag this new thing back into their old world.)

Because Airbnb's POV changed the premise.

Anytime a company begins its journey rooted in the past, it is making the unconscious, undiscussed, unquestioned decision to "accept the way it is," in no way challenging the current paradigm on any meaningful level. As a result, its POV, and everything written and communicated emerges from this perspective: "We accept the way things are today, and our goal is to help make today *better, faster, cheaper*, tomorrow."

All of that screams one thing and one thing only:

You are not creating an exponentially different future.

You are Blockbuster, but *better*.

Instead, here's how Category Designers think:

It's tomorrow.

The world is not the same way it was yesterday.

We REJECT the premise. And we are going to act as if the tomorrow we're creating already exists, today.

Our friend, Mike Maples Jr., calls this "Backcasting."

> "*Legendary builders must stand in the future and pull the present from the current reality to the future of their design. People living in the present usually dislike breakthrough ideas when they first hear about them. They have no context for what will be radically different in the future. So an important additional job of the builder is to persuade early like-minded people to join a new movement.*"

And how do you give people context that excites them enough to meet you in the future and join your new movement?

You give them a new Point Of View they can grab onto—and can repeat to their friends, who will tell their friends, and so on, and so on.

Pirates reject the premise.

Of course, when you introduce a new POV to the world, what happens?

99% of the time, you get criticized—which is exactly what happened to Picasso.

> *"Early Cubist paintings were often misunderstood by critics and viewers because they were thought to be merely geometric art. Yet the painters themselves believed they were presenting a new kind of reality that broke away from Renaissance tradition, especially from the use of perspective and illusion."*

The most effective POVs aim the conversation in such a different direction that it's oftentimes difficult for the masses to understand (or accept) what this new POV might mean for the world.

Here are a few powerful examples:

"Gay rights."

These two words reveal a radically different Point Of View of the world—of which many (diseased) folks have a very hard time accepting.

"Equal pay for equal work."

There was a time in history where *it was the law* that men and women did not earn the same amount of money.

Then, a new POV was introduced, adopted, and "The Equal Pay Act" was signed in 1963.

"Undocumented Citizens"

In 2021, the Biden administration ordered U.S. immigration enforcement agencies to change how they talk about immigrants. Why? Because words matter. And referring to immigrants as "illegal aliens" reinforces (at scale) one POV—whereas "undocumented noncitizen" reinforces another. *"This is part of a broader effort by the Biden administration to... build what they call a more 'humane' immigration system."*

The current U.S. government is doing something that has never been done before: distinguishing "illegal aliens" from migrants on the southern border begging for asylum.

They're two different types of people.

(We are not expressing anything political here. We're just underscoring how POVs work at both the societal and business level. Because human beings respond to POVs.)

"Don't Go There, Live There"

This Airbnb tagline is a POV. And it changes everything. Airbnb did not say, "We're better than hotels." They attacked the old category ("being a tourist") by creating a different category that produced a different experience. And once people saw this legendary, different POV, they couldn't unsee it.

Airbnb stopped people in their tracks: "I never thought about travel like that." And with their category designing POV, they executed a Dam The Demand strategy against hotels. (And made hotel owners damn mad. *Arrrrr!*)

In order to change the world, and unlock exponential breakthroughs, you have to reject the premise.

You can't start with impressionism and aim to make it better.

You have to Stop. Change. And Start again.

You have to invent cubism.

Here's how:

Category Design + POV + Languaging

What creates the category is your POV.

And what crystalizes your POV is Languaging.

Let's walk through how this works.

Step 1: (Category) Design The Future

An easy way of understanding whether you are accepting or rejecting the premise is by questioning whether you are Forecasting or Backcasting. Which direction are you facing?

- **Forecasting**: Standing in the past, looking forward, thinking about the future.
- **Backcasting**: Standing in a different future, and living "as if" that different future already exists today.

This might seem like an inconsequential nuance, BUT, it is the starting point that defines the entire trajectory of your creative act and/or company. If you start with the way the world "is," and then try to make the way it "is," *better*, you are making an unconscious decision to improve within the context of a game someone else invented.

You are competing.

But if you start with the way it "could be," if you assume the possible and stand in the future, you give yourself the opportunity to write new rules to the new game you are inventing.

You are unencumbered by the past and present.

You are creating.

Forecasting or Backcasting is what decides whether you are creating a new category (and then educating people on the new and different benefits that get unlocked as a result) or competing within an existing category (and emphasizing why the benefits you provide customers/consumers/users are "better").

Step 2: Visit The Future For POV Hypotheses

How do you visit the future? Let us show you the lenses that let you take a sneak peak.

Do our category's customers have "Stockholm Syndrome"? Can we set them free?

Stockholm Syndrome is when abuse victims and captives have positive feelings towards their abusers/captors. Well, the same can be said for customers, consumers, and users who become so desensitized to the negative experiences familiar to the existing category that they stop wondering what else might be possible if these negative experiences never existed in the first place.

If you can design and free customers from the "abuse" they've grown accustomed to in the "old" category, you will have an amazing POV for a new and different category.

If Michael Lewis, Malcolm Gladwell, Doris Kearns Goodwin, and Bob Woodward wrote a book about your category... what would they say?

Imagine what breakthrough insight one of these legendary authors may reveal to the world, fundamentally changing the way the masses thought about your category of "thing." What truths would they uncover? Who would be their heroes and villains? What might they write that would make all the incumbents hang their heads in shame? What could they write that might bring us to tears of gratitude that someone noticed? What would the verdict of history be?

Say that.

That's a POV worth sharing with the world.

What does the category look like if you gave your Superconsumers infinite power & resources?

What would a "cleaning Superconsumer" do with unlimited power and resources? Probably create a daily hotel cleaning service for their home? Well, that's the POV of an iRobot Roomba, where you can clean your house every day (or several times a day if you wanted) with the tap on your phone.

What would a "coffee Superconsumer" do with unlimited power and resources? Maybe hire a personal Barista at home? Isn't that what Keurig does today, providing hundreds of choices of coffee so you can pick what you want, when you want it?

What would a "music Superconsumer" do with unlimited power and resources? Create a device to hold 1,000 songs in their pocket (the original iPod)? Create a database with access to millions of songs streamed at their pleasure (Apple Music)?

To imagine the future **unconstrained from the past**, play The Breakthrough Game from the perspective of your Superconsumers with unlimited power & resources, and you will catch a glimpse of the future.

Step 3: Write Your POV

Once you've glimpsed the future, you need to plant your flag and tell people how the future will be different.

It's time to write your POV.

Now, we want to be very clear about something: a quippy tagline doesn't mean you have a POV. The vast majority of companies and creators unconsciously choose to compete within existing categories rather than create new ones. Then, they compound the stupidity by pairing their undifferentiated category with a *meaningless* tagline.

Here's the proof:

New Thinking, New Possibilities

Whose tagline is this? Maybe it's a Think Tank? An innovation lab? NASA? A neuroscience institute? Maybe it's the tagline for a new Alzheimer's drug?

Actually, it's Hyundai—a South Korean multinational automotive manufacturer.

This, by the way, is the "new and improved" version of their old tagline, which was "Drive Your Way." As if, in a brand new Range Rover, you don't get to "Drive Your Way." New Ferrari? You don't get to "Drive Your Way" either. New BMW? New Mercedes? Nope, it's only Hyundai where you get to "Drive Your Way."

It means nothing.

More importantly, this tagline does not reflect any new and different POV customers can grab onto, internalize, and then use as the script to tell their friends and family what makes Hyundai "DIFFERENT."

Here's another one.

Run Simple

Whose tagline is this?

Maybe it's an athleisure company? Or maybe it's a company that makes jockstraps? Or groin cream? Anti-chafing boxers?

Actually, it's SAP—a German enterprise resource planning software company.

Then (if you want your head to really explode), after *running* with that tagline for a while, they decided to change it to: "The Best Run."

Listen to the words. "We accept the way the world is, and we want to help you do what you're already doing, better." They probably spent $10 million and 11 months hiring Whoever & Whoever (a subdivision advertising agency under WPP) helping them come up with that. And it means nothing.

No new "different" POV.

What makes this even more insane is that SAP's customers (for the most part) are large, multinational corporations. The last thing they are is "simple." They are massively complex. Simplicity is in no way what they want in ERP software. What they want is the ability to effectively, with precision, run gigantic omnichannel, multicountry, multi-currency, multi-business-model, complex-multi-product/serviceline, complex-eco-system and multi-business-unit businesses (say that five times fast). Nothing about what these megaprises want is simple.

Instead, SAP is unconsciously announcing to the world, "We do the same thing as everybody else, but we're the best."

OK, so what happens when Oracle says they're the best, and Salesforce says they're the best, and everybody else says they're the best?

Then who is the best?

The rule of thumb here is that if your tagline, and subsequent POV can easily work for someone else, that means you don't have a POV.

You have a meaningless brand and tagline (that could be used by lots of other companies).

Meanwhile, Substack's POV ("A place for independent writing") wouldn't work for *The New York Times*. And that's the point. That's why Substack is seen as "different." Because they don't see the world the same way.

Another example, and one of Pirate Cole's personal favorite POVs is Vinebox: "Premium wine by the glass."

Notice how the tagline isn't really "a tagline" in the way the marketing world loves giggling over clever puns and inane throw away nursery rhyme sayings. It's actually the company's POV. "We believe premium wines are delicious, but committing to buy an entire bottle of premium wine only to not enjoy what you've just bought is a terrible experience. So instead, we ship you vials of premium wine by the glass—and then any you really like, you can buy a full bottle of as well."

That's a radically different POV!

"Premium wine by the glass" doesn't work for 99% of wine manufacturers, all of whom sell *bottles of wine*. In fact, if you were a marketing executive in the room and you suggested this POV and tagline, you would be met with hostile rejection. "What are you crazy?! We can't sell our wine by the glass. We sell it by the bottle, you idiot!"

The number of people Pirate Cole has told about Vinebox is astonishing. And every single time, he repeats the same phrase over and over again—which is the script the company gave to him. "Oh, it's premium wine by the glass. You order a box, they send you a bunch of vials of different wines, and then you can do a wine tasting at home."

Pirate Cole isn't just doing "word-of-mouth marketing" for Vinebox.

He is *repeating and scaling* the POV of the company. (FYI: Pirate Christopher would never buy from Vinebox because he thinks wine makers should make the bottles BIGGER and can't understand why anyone would want *just a glass!?*.... Different categories, different Superconsumers.)

This same foundational principle is true for all products and services, works of art, physical and metaphysical objects—anything in the world we give "value."

For example, in the enterprise software category where Pirate Christopher grew up, most "buyers" issue RFPs (Request For Proposals) to "vendors" in a given category.

This is the B2B equivalent of the muscle man bikini contest.

- Buyer issues an RFP.
- Vendors respond to the RFP.
- All the vendors compete against each other for the business ("Pick me! Pick me!").
- One vendor "wins."

But any good enterprise tech salesperson knows there are two kinds of vendors.

- The vendor (singular) that helps the customer write the RFP.
- And the vendors (plural) that respond to the RFP.

Can you guess who wins the business?

The person who writes the RFP with the customer—because they're best "positioned" to respond to their own "Request For Proposals."

So think of your POV as the RFP for the whole category. And this is true both in B2B and B2C.

Your POV becomes the raison d'etre for why customers are doing and spending what they are doing and spending. ("Don't go there, live there.") Your POV is the True North justification for why customers are making the investment they are making. (Either to their spouse in B2C or boss in B2B). And a powerful category POV is the radically different "air cover" that ground troops (salespeople) need in order to get into sales opportunities. For example, Salesforce's sales reps never had to deal with buyers who thought the Cloud was a stupid idea. Because the "No Software" POV attracted visionary customers and repelled buyers who "needed" to own the software. Same for AirBnB. These are legendary examples of "making the market come to you" vs "go-to-market." And category POV marketing (vs "I'm better than you" brand marketing) tends to lower the cost of customer acquisition—because the sales teams deal almost exclusively with prospects who "get it."

How To Create Your POV.

"If I had an hour to solve a problem, I'd spend 55 minutes thinking about the problem and five minutes thinking about solutions." —Albert Einstein

Legendary POVs have a simple architecture.

Frame a different problem/opportunity.

Most people point to the "No Software" POV as a strategic component of Salesforce's success in designing a category. And it was. But most people also forget that Salesforce successfully Framed, Named, and Claimed the problem with the old category as well—and they did so with new languaging.

They called the old thing "On premise."

SAP and Siebel didn't call their stuff "on premise." Salesforce re-framed the old category with a functionally correct, *new* description, and then imbued "on premise" with massive negative connotations. "You don't want 'on premise' do you?" (As if they were saying, "You don't want genital bacterial leprosy, do you?")

Netflix did exactly the same thing in the B2C space, calling "appointment viewing" a massive problem. "Why wait until Thursday at 8pm to watch what you want to watch? You should be able to watch TV when *you* want to!"

The magic combination of Category Design is both Naming & Claiming the future (where you are going), as well as the past ("you don't want that old thing, do you?").

Evangelize a different future.

When Pirate Christopher was CMO of enterprise software juggernaut, Mercury, they created the "Business Technology Optimization" category (BTO) with the POV "Run IT Like A Business."

The idea was: if Enterprise Resource Planning (ERP) is about optimizing the "back-end" of the business, and Customer Relationship Management (CRM) is about optimizing the "front-end" of the business, then BTO is about optimizing the "business of IT."

Thus, "Run IT Like A Business."

This immediately made Mercury the company that could help CIOs deliver business outcomes (vs technical "IT outcomes"), and put Mercury's competitors into a nit-norky technical box they could never get out of. The BTO POV not only created a category for Mercury to dominate, it also gave customers a mantra—a rally cry and reason to do things differently.

The moment your POV becomes an agenda item for your customers, you know you have something.

Show customers how your "solution" bridges the gap from the problem/opportunity to the different future.

"Take one 5-Hour Energy and it won't feel like 2:30 anymore."

5 Hour Energy's early marketing is a great example of legendary category marketing with a legendary POV. All in 30 seconds.

Pirate Cole did the same thing with his ghostwriting & thought leadership agency, Digital Press. Instead of selling "blog posts," his business sold the outcome of "thought leadership"—which solves a very different problem and unlocks a very different future than, "We need content for our company blog."

As a result, "thought leadership" became an agenda item on every company's Marketing To Do list. And in 2 years, Pirate Cole's agency wrote on behalf of more than 300 company executives, Silicon Valley startups, angel investors, venture capitalists, and more.

Instead, most marketers think tactically:

"I should buy Google ads."

But almost no one asks, strategically, "What makes a customer Google something in the first place?"

The answer is a POV.

POVs cause lightbulbs to go off in consumers' heads, and to consider the new and different.

"Hey I've been hearing about cloud databases....I need to check that out...I'm going to Google the words 'Cloud Database.'

Or, in the B2C space: *"WOW... an eBike?.... I need to check that out....I'm going to Google this new word 'eBike' I just heard."*

Most importantly, the company that evangelizes the POV is immediately viewed as the leader. Because the only companies customers have ever seen market the category (and not the brand: "We're the best!") is the category leader.

A few other POV favorites of ours:

- **Keurig:** "Single-serve coffee." It's not a cup of coffee you buy from a coffee shop. It's not a pot of coffee you find leftover in the office kitchen. It's a pod you put in a device and voila: a single cup of fresh, hot coffee—made just for you, by you.

- **iRobot:** "Robot vacuum cleaner." It's not a vacuum cleaner "with more horsepower." It's not a vacuum cleaner with more knobs, bells, suction tubes, and whistles. It's a vacuum cleaner that doesn't require you to vacuum on a daily basis. WOW!

- **Royal Canin:** "Tailored health nutrition for cats & dogs." It's not "better" dog and cat food. It's *personalized* dog and cat food that is breed specific. *It's a different thing.*

- **Slo Axe:** "Mobile Axe Throwing." Why go to an axe throwing bar (a legendary new category in itself!) when the axe throwing can come to you! (Pirate Christopher's family just did this and it was a blast.)

Step 4: Languaging

Most companies don't design new categories.

Even fewer design new categories and then consciously, intentionally, and carefully construct a POV customers/consumers/users can hear once, internalize, and then repeat to their friends and family.

But the most legendary companies do both of the above, plus one more step:

They invent new language for the new POV and new category of "thing" they are creating.

This is what we call Languaging: the strategic use of language to change thinking.

- **Sushirrito:** "The original sushi burrito." It's not sushi. And it's not a burrito. Calling it a "sushi burrito" would have been enough to get the point across, but they went a step further and used Languaging *to create a new word for their new thing.* Because they are different and solve a different problem: How do you eat sushi on the go? A "Sushirrito" is NOT easily replaceable or comparable with a regular sushi restaurant that competes on price, quality, and location.

- **Selfie:** It's a picture of yourself, taken by yourself. But it's not enough to just say, "It's a picture of yourself, taken by yourself." The idea *sticks* and *spreads* when you use Languaging and CALL IT SOMETHING DIFFER-ENT. "A picture of yourself, taken by yourself, *is called a...* Selfie."

- **The Tipping Point:** This group of words is defined by Malcolm Gladwell to mean, "That magic moment when an idea, trend, or social behavior crosses a threshold, tips, and spreads like wildfire." But just saying that isn't what makes the idea *stick.* What makes it stick is taking that idea and then calling it something new and different. That magic moment? That moment is called "The Tipping Point."
- **Dynamic Data Exchange (DDE):** This communication protocol lets applications "call" each other, which Microsoft created as a critical technical criteria for products in the "Productivity Suite" category.
- **Secure Sockets Layer (SSL)** This is a protocol named and developed by Netscape for establishing an encrypted link between a web server and a browser. SSL became an industry standard for transmitting private data securely, in part because Netscape made it a priority through new Languaging.

In technical/technology oriented categories, new standards, protocols, architectures, and frameworks matter. A ton. And to make new technical standards stick, you need to create new languaging standards. (Just like Starbucks did in the B2C space with "Grande Latte.")

The reason new languaging works is simple:

You can't use old words to describe new things. People don't buy it.

Languaging, in the context of category design and writing the POV of the company, can either take the form of 1) inventing new words and/ or language for the new ideas you are looking to communicate, or 2) modifying old words with new words for the new ideas you are looking to communicate.

- "Sushirito" is a new word.

- "Selfie" is a new word.
- "Electric Car" is an old word (Car) modified with a new word (Electric).
- "Cryptocurrency" is an old word (Currency) modified with a new word (Crypto).

What creates the category is your new and different POV.

And what crystalizes your POV is Languaging.

This is how people "get" what you're talking about.

Everything else is just *better/faster/cheaper/smarter/stronger* noise.

CHAPTER SIX

Languaging

The Strategic Use Of Language To Change Thinking

Category Design is a game of thinking.

You are responsible for changing the way a reader, customer, consumer, or user "thinks." And you are successful when you've moved their thinking *from* the old way *to the new and different way* you are educating them about.

The way you do this is with words.

Which means if you can't write what you're thinking, then you aren't thinking clearly. And if you aren't thinking clearly, then how are you going to change the way the reader, customer, consumer, or user thinks?

In various Category Pirates letters, we have written about the different levers you can push and pull to differentiate your business (and even how to differentiate yourself in your career). But how you get customers to understand what *makes* you different, how you get readers hooked on your content, how you get investors to understand why you're moving from one profit model to another (like Adobe did), and how you get employees, team members, and fellow executives to align their efforts (aka: align their *thinking*) is by using very specific, very intentional language. (At first blush, it's hard to be against something called, "The Clean Air Act." *That's on purpose.*)

The strategic use of language to change thinking is called Languaging.

We believe this is one of the most under-discussed, unexamined aspects of business & marketing today.

- When President Biden orders U.S. immigration enforcement agencies to change how they talk about immigrants and change terms like "Illegal Alien" to "Undocumented Noncitizen," **that's languaging.**
- When the dairy industry spends 100 years educating the general public that milk comes from cows, and then someone comes along and introduces "Almond Milk" (or Oat Milk, or Flax Milk), **that's languaging.**
- When the whole world understands what an acoustic guitar is, and Les Paul comes along and starts wailing away on an "Electric Guitar," **that's languaging.**
- Languaging is about creating distinctions between old and new, same and different.

Legendary Category Designers are languaging masters.

A demarcation point in language creates a demarcation point in thinking, creates a demarcation point in action, creates a demarcation point in outcome.

When Henry Ford called the first vehicle a "horseless carriage," he was using language to get the customer to STOP, listen, and immediately understand the FROM-TO: the way the world was *to the new and different way he wanted it to be.* Had he called the first vehicle a "faster horse," that would have been lazy languaging (and lazy thinking).

And it all starts with your POV.

Your Point Of View Of The Category Is What "Hooks" The Customer

The language you use reflects your Point Of View.

And your Point Of View frames a new problem and a new solution in a provocative way.

If marketing is your ability to evangelize a new category, and branding is how well you can associate your product with the benefits of the category, then languaging is how you market the category, and your brand within that category, *based on your company's unwavering, unquestionably unique point of view.*

You can tell when a company doesn't have a unique POV of their category when their "messages" conflict with one another, have unclarified and "weak" aims, or worst of all, have no clear aim at all. Today they're evangelizing one category, tomorrow they're evangelizing a different category (all the while thinking they are "trying out different marketing & messaging phrases").

For example, a cereal company might run one advertisement saying,

"The healthiest way to start the day!" The very next campaign, however, they might change the message to, "A healthy breakfast alternative." What's the cereal company's unwavering POV of the category? Is it that breakfast *is* the best way to start the day—and they're the solution?

Or is it that breakfast *isn't* the best way to start the day—and they're the solution?

Frame it, Name it, and Claim it.

Companies and creators with unclarified, undefined POVs eventually come to the conclusion that they have a problem (sales are down, attention is sparse). But they end up stating the root of their problem in the way they ask for help: "We need to work on our messaging." More times than not, what they mean when they say "messaging" isn't actually *messaging*—but category point of view.

Most messaging is meaningless, context free, point of view-less, forgettable garbage. "Experience amazing," "Imagination at work," "That's what I like," "Run simple," are taglines for who? Don't know? Neither does anyone else. (Lexus. GE. Pepsi. SAP.)

The reason this clarity is so important, and why we want to draw lines in the sand between category point of view, languaging, and messaging, is because improving a company's messaging *in absence of a true north category POV* is a (and we use this word very intentionally) "meaningless," money burning project.

- A POV is, "What do we stand for?"
- Languaging is, "How do we powerfully communicate our POV?"
- And messaging is, "What should we say?"

Well, how can you possibly know what to say unless you know what you stand for? What difference do you make in the world? What problem do you solve?

Your point of view should be well defined and chiseled into the company's tablets, with intentionally chosen words that reflect the company's POV, so the true science of messaging can begin: a never-ending experiment of swapping in and out of words, phrases, promotions, testimonials, and other "messages" in order to figure out which are (another very intentional word here) *resonating* and most effectively evangelizing your category POV.

And it all starts with how you choose to Frame, Name, and Claim the problem.

For example, there's a reason why men have "erectile dysfunction" and not "impotence."

Impotence has very negative implications attached to the word. If a man says he is impotent, it's as though he has a character flaw. It means "not manly" or "unable to be a man." That's not a word very many men want to be associated with—meaning men don't want to admit to having such a problem. (Hard to sell a solution to a problem no one wants to admit to having!)

In order to solve this problem, Pfizer (the makers of Viagra) *had to invent a disease*, called "erectile dysfunction," to make impotence a more approachable problem. And then they shortened it to "ED" to make it even softer and safer to associate with. It's a whole lot easier for a man to say, "I am experiencing ED" than to say "I am impotent."

This is what languaging does.

It changes the way people perceive the thing they're looking at.

Netflix is another legendary example.

Their POV is that you should be able to watch anything you want, whenever you want. That's the "frame" of the problem. They then Name & Claim the solution to that problem: "streaming."

But what Netflix also did was also Frame, Name, and Claim the OLD category experience too. And they did so in a way that was functionally accurate and simultaneously spelled out the problem immediately for customers. They called it "appointment viewing."

In order for "streaming" and on-demand to work, you also have to believe "appointment viewing" is a problem. And nobody in the 90s and 2000s thought "appointment viewing" was a problem. You just assumed you could only watch what you wanted to watch at the hour it was on. As a result, the language people used back then when asking their friends and family about a new TV show was, "When is it on?"

This phrase, *this language,* no longer exists.

Today, we don't ask, "When is it on?" The new category overtook the old category—which means new language replaces the old language. Now we ask, "*What* is it on? Netflix? Disney+? Hulu?"

Whoever Frames & Names the problem Claims the language—and wins.

And it's the POV and the language you use to reflect that POV that makes your "messaging" inspire customers to take action.

Not the other way around.

In your marketing, branding, product descriptions, etc., language has the potential to reflect the unspoken qualities of your category point of view. Our good friend, Lee Hartley Carter, communication expert and author of *Persuasion: Convincing Others When Facts Don't Seem To Matter,* refers to this as "the understanding that language has the power to create thinking, which in turn inspires action."

For example, when you walk into a coffee shop, *any coffee shop other than Starbucks,* what words do coffee drinkers frequently use to order their coffee? "Hi, I'd like a double grande latte please." But "Grande" isn't the universal word for "medium." It's Starbucks' word, which a good chunk of the category has adopted. Strarbucks would never have succeeded unless they designed their own category lexicon. Especially when asked to pay $4.00 for a coffee. But customers do it every day—because they aren't spending $4.00 for "coffee." They're spending $4.00 for fancy "Grande" coffee.

Another genius of Starbucks category languaging is that their words are new, fresh, and yet familiar at the same time. The first time we hear, "Venti Mocha," we have an idea what that might mean. Even though we had never heard it before.

Category queens deliberately use languaging to do a few things:

1. To differentiate themselves from any and all competition through word choice, tone, and nuance.

2. To speak to (and speak "like") the customers they want to attract—especially the Superconsumers of the category.

3. To further establish their position in the category they are designing or redesigning.

4. To insinuate and give context to other levers of differentiation: price, profit model, branding, etc., and how the company executes any number of them *in a different way.*

Languaging can be applied to all 8 levers of category differentiation:

If you want to put your company's POV to the test, walk through the following 8 levers and question how intentionally you are using language to educate customers on the differences between the new category you are creating and the old category that currently exists.

Languaging helps you name the category you are creating (by framing a different problem with a different benefit): There are cars, and then there are *electric* cars. There's digital marketing, and then there is *chatbot* marketing.

Languaging is how you write a compelling mission statement for your brand: Apple's "Think Different" is a great example (which works because the proper way to say that is, of course, "Think Differently"). Changing the word to the grammatically incorrect "different" forces the reader to stop. This is intentional language that ties the audience of the new category and the mission statement of the brand together.

Languaging educates the customer on the experience you are proposing: *Streaming* video implies a very different experience than getting in your car, driving to your local Blockbuster, and *renting* a video. Same goes for today's *contactless* pick-up at grocery stores and restaurants versus standard "pick-up" practices.

Languaging frames the perceived value of your product or service: A medium coffee is perceived to be cheap, but a *Grande* coffee is perceived to be expensive.

Languaging hints at the benefits that come with radically different manufacturing: An *eBook* is a dematerialized book. It can be produced infinitely, distributed infinitely, edited and uploaded in an instant, etc. One single letter "e" tells customers, "This thing isn't created, distributed, or consumed the same way regular "books" are."

Languaging also hints at the benefits that come with radically different distribution: OnlyFans call creators who invite other creators to the platform using their referral link "Referred Creators," which signals the benefits of their flywheel and the money you can earn as a result.

Languaging is the "hook" customers, consumers, and users latch onto in your marketing: Substack's *paid* newsletters are a different thing than Mailchimp's *free* newsletters. Marketing something fundamentally different is always easier and more enticing to the customer than trying to market something that is "better" than what currently exists, but still *the same kind of thing*.

Languaging also signals to customers how to think about paying for your product or service: Paying a *subscription* is different from buying products individually. Or purchasing *in-game items* inside a free video game is different from playing a *freemium* game with ads. (These are all words and phrases that did not exist until a decade ago, and were purposely used to design new categories.)

Too many marketers, executives, founders, and even venture capital firms think the words a company uses are all about "standing out."

But you can't stand out without a clear and different POV. Lexus can scream "Experience Amazing" all it wants and most people will never be able to recall those words and connect them to their brand. Because they do not frame a problem.

You can't stand out if your POV isn't being communicated through intentional languaging.

In fact, "languaging" is often more about who the brand, product, and company is NOT for than who the brand *is* for. The more directly you can speak to the people you are trying to help most, the more likely it is for them to see you as the "undeniable champion" solution of the category you are creating. But the moment you try to widen your net (purely for the sake of "going after a bigger audience"), you begin to dilute your language. Your words become generalized and vague. Because you aren't speaking to any "one" person. And if you keep going, and widen your company's language to be "something for everything," all of your messaging ends up being another frequency wave that sits in the never-ending hum of white noise—something for no one. (SAP's message is meaningingful to no one: "Run Simple.")

When languaging is executed successfully, and is reflective of a well-defined POV of the category, two things happen.

1. You become known for the new language you've invented.

You know your languaging is working when customers start using the language you created.

For example, in the early 2000s, Salesforce founder, Marc Benioff, created new language for the category he was creating. He called it "cloud-based software." (There's "software" you buy and install on your computer via CD-ROM, and there's "cloud-based software" you buy and use from any computer, and any browser, connected to the Internet.)

In addition, and to further "twist the knife" into the backs of his competitors, he also invented language to reframe the way people thought about the *old* category by referring to it as "on-premise software." Notice the distinction: "On-premise software" runs on computers on the premises of the person or organization using the software. "Cloud-based software" runs on a remote facility outside the organization.

What happened?

The entire technology industry started adopting the language he and Salesforce invented.

2. Customers don't see you as "better." They see you as different.

The second thing that happens when you successfully use language to change thinking is you Dam The Demand.

When you use intentional language to modify the existing category ("cloud-based software"), you create a chasm between the old and the new. For example, an "e-bike" is not *better* than a "bicycle." It's something different. It has different benefits, different use cases, even different price points, profit models, and manufacturing processes. One single letter and a dash tells the reader/customer/consumer/user "this thing is not like what came before it." Same goes for "frozen food" and "fresh food," or "sunglasses" and "glasses." These languaging modifications make the customer STOP, tilt their head, and immediately wonder, "This is for something different—do I need this?"

And since you were the one who invented the language, you become the trusted authority to educate them on the definition of that new language—and subsequently, that new category.

Languaging is how you change the world.

At the highest level, languaging is used to move society forward.

Not long ago, people living on the streets were called "whinos" and "bumbs." Today, they are called, "people experiencing homelessness." This new languaging changes how people perceive the problem and subsequently treat others and work toward a solution.

Remember: A demarcation point in language creates a demarcation point in thinking, creates a demarcation point in action, creates a demarcation point in outcome.

There was also a point in time when the legal minimum wage for women was lower than it was for men. Women got paid less. Until a movement mobilized around some strategic, future-changing languaging: "Equal pay for equal work." And these words were so powerful, they changed the *law*.

And sometimes, languaging emerges through new combinations of words into a portmanteau.

- Gamification
- Infotainment

- Brunch
- Podcast
- Frenemy

Whenever language is bent, it tweaks the ear to listen—and to consider the *different*.

We all have AIDS.

In 2005, fashion designer, Kenneth Cole, launched an AIDS awareness campaign in conjunction with the American Foundation for AIDS Research.

The POV was: "We All Have AIDS... If One Of Us Does."

Notice, this is not "a clever message." This is a radically different, crystal clear point of view of the world, reflected through languaging: the strategic use of language to change thinking.

The campaign then featured figures such as former South African President Nelson Mandela, South African advocate Zackie Achmat, South African Archbishop Desmond Tutu, as well as actresses Ashley Judd, Sharon Stone, and Elizabeth Taylor, and actors Tom Hanks, Will Smith, and so on, all with the chief aim of minimizing the stigma associated with the disease. Kenneth Cole & the American Foundation for AIDS Research wanted to dispel the myth that AIDS is only an issue for HIV-positive people.

How?

By saying, very clearly, "If anyone is infected, we are all affected. If it exists anywhere, it exists everywhere."

Now that's a POV!

Languaging + Math = Story Arc.

If languaging is how you communicate your differentiated POV, then numbers are how you communicate the urgency of your POV.

Numbers are what give your story an arc.

In everything you say, you are either communicating one of two story arcs. Either you have no treasure, and you've found a map that says there's lots of treasure *over there*. Or, you're Chicken Little with lots of treasure warning everyone the sky is falling. Numbers are the evidence, and amplify the language.

To be clear, we're not saying you need to understand how to perform statistical analyses or do napkin calculus. (Pirate Christopher failed 3rd-grade math, and Pirate Cole still counts with his fingers.) Languaging masters simply need to understand whether something small today could be gargantuan tomorrow, or something big today could be small, even nonexistent tomorrow—and then strategically use language to educate readers, listeners, customers, and consumers on the importance of that story arc.

The Origin Story of McKinsey

For example, McKinsey & Company was a firm founded in 1926 by James O. McKinsey, a University of Chicago accounting professor. McKinsey started out as a group of bean counters and accountants, not the defacto standard of world-class professional services we associate today with McKinsey.

Who built McKinsey into the powerhouse firm it became was Marvin Bower, the Harvard Law School and Harvard Business School graduate hired by James O. McKinsey. And Bower had a powerful ah-ha. He discovered a "missing." He noticed that while clients paid for accounting services, what they often valued more was business advice from a trusted source.

Mavin Bower is the category designer of *management* consulting.

He was a languaging maniac.

Under his guide, projects were not called "jobs." They were *engagements*—a word that is much more relational than transactional. Internal groups with specific industry or functional expertise were called *practices (Like doctors, this is the intentional use of language to create the perception of value)*—emphasizing that learning was a never-ending endeavor. Finally, McKinsey was not a "business." It was a *firm*—highlighting the core values that held the company together. Even today there are few firms who are as rigorously committed (some might say cultishly committed) to the original language Marvin Bower put into place.

All these distinctions helped McKinsey thrive and create the $255 billion-dollar global category known today as Management Consulting. And notice: history remembers the lawyer, Marvin Bower (lawyers are trained in the discipline of language), not the accountant, as the "father of management consulting."

All legendary languaging represents 1 of 4 math equations:

- Addition
- Subtraction
- Multiplication
- Division

If your languaging does not tell one of these 4 story arcs, no one is going to listen to what you have to say. There is no urgency. You are responsible not just for strategically using new words to frame new problems (or reframe old problems), but to also reveal whether the slope is positive or negative—are the numbers going up or down? Where is this story going? And your ability to comprehend and communicate that slope is what makes your languaging matter.

Addition: "With C4 pre-workout, your workouts will *last longer.*"

Subtraction: "With Spanx, pounds seemingly *disappear.* A flat stomach *in seconds.*"

Multiplication: "With an acoustic guitar, only some people can hear your music. With an electric guitar, *an entire stadium of people* can hear your music."

Division: "Condoms are 98% effective at *protecting against and reducing the spread of* most STDs."

The power of languaging is multiplied (pun intended) when paired with numbers.

Because numbers tell powerful stories too.

So as you sail forward in life and business, we ask that you pay special attention to the Framing, Naming, and Claiming of things. Because we get taught to think by the words people use with us (which means you can teach others to think by the words you use with them).

Peter Drucker is considered one of the greatest management "thinkers" of all time.

He is best known for being a distinguished teacher—first as Professor of Politics and Philosophy at Bennington College, then as Professor of Management at the Graduate Business School of New York University, and Clarke Professor of Social Science at Claremont Graduate School in California. But if there is one overarching concept Drucker is best known for, it's his belief that every person was responsible for his or her own acquisition of learning.

How Drucker did this himself was through writing.

He is the author of 39 books, including the best-seller (must read), *The Effective Executive*. He also held a column in the Wall Street Journal for more than a decade—while also frequently contributing work to *Harvard Business Review, The Atlantic, and The Economist*. By the end of his lifetime, his writings had been translated into more than 36 different languages, and been read all over the world.

So why did Drucker write so much, if he was really a teacher and educator first?

Because writing was his way of clarifying his thinking.

Most writers spend their entire careers thinking in the context of "better."

Writing education programs promise to help you become a "better" writer.

Agents and publishers encourage writers to (this drives us mad), "Mention books similar to yours" when trying to land a book deal.

Conventional wisdom in the world of words is that in order to "make it" as a writer, you need to find what worked for someone else and then *do that.* Or, find what worked for someone else and then do the same thing, *but better.* (Good luck being a "better" writer than Shakespeare, Dickens, or Dickinson.)

In reality, this advice is why the vast majority of writers live in poverty.

According to the *New York Times, "The median pay for full-time writers was $20,300 in 2017, and that number decreased to $6,080 when part-time writers were considered. The latter figure reflects a 42% drop since 2009, when the median was $10,500. These findings are the result of an expansive 2018 study of more than 5,000 published book authors, across genres and including both traditional and self-published writers."*

What studies like these fail to take into account, however, is that hierarchies and social class structures only exist in "better" games. Measuring the median pay for full-time writers only matters if you want to be "better" than the competition. But "better" is rarely what unlocks exponential rewards for writers (or for anyone, in any industry).

Instead, your goal as a writer should be to *be different.*

More specifically, your goal should be to illustrate different *think-ing*—not just say what has already been said, "better." Drucker wasn't a "better" management writer. His point of view was that "big business and nonprofit enterprises were the defining innovation of the 20th century," which led him to pioneer social and management theories that ended up changing the way the world thought about work, teams, business responsibilities, labor leverage, laws, and more. He was even the one to Frame, Name, and Claim the term "knowledge worker"—meaning laborers who do not use their hands, but their minds in combination with scalable technologies.

Peter Drucker wouldn't have become "Peter Drucker" had he regurgitated the same old, same old "management best practices" that came before him, "better." No matter how talented of a technical writer he may have been.

The reason he became THE ONE AND ONLY "Peter Drucker" is because he was not easily compared to anyone already in the category of business writer.

Because if you are comparable, that also means you're replaceable.

And if you're easily replaceable, then you're one of the many writers who fade into nothingness (and end up earning less than minimum wage for your work in the process).

Frame it, Name it, and Claim it.

Most writers don't realize that differentiation in writing has very little to do with the actual words on the page, and has everything to do with the words you use to illustrate different thinking.

For example, *The Tipping Point* by Malcolm Gladwell is one of the best-selling books of our time, and has sold more than 3 million copies to date. The book is about "that magic moment when an idea, trend, or social behavior crosses a threshold, **tips**, and spreads like wildfire." Said differently, the book is basically an explanation of how word-of-mouth marketing works.

Is that a novel idea?

Not really. There are lots of books on "word-of-mouth" and even more on "marketing."

What made it seem novel was the new & specific language (the Framing, Naming, and Claiming) Gladwell used to redefine (or redesign) the topic. Had Gladwell been playing the "better" game, as so many writers often do, the title of his book likely would have been something like: *Better, Faster Word-Of-Mouth Marketing.* He'd have fallen right into the "better" trap, and likely become a statistic: "*The median pay for full-time writers was $20,300 in 2017.*"

The nuance here most people fail to notice is that Gladwell successfully created a new term for an old idea. And in doing so, he became known as "The Tipping Point guy," first, and "a really great writer," second. And if you take Gladwell's MasterClass, you will learn some pretty cool things about how to improve your writing (that is to say: become a "better" writer). But what you will not learn is how Malcolm became "Malcolm Gladwell"—which happened by using languaging to give this familiar, unoriginal idea a new definition.

He called it something *different.*

He made it fresh and "new."

And since he was the one to create the distinction, he became known for the idea—which, to a reader, appears as *different thinking.* Say "The Tipping Point," and someone in the room will undoubtedly say, "You've read Malcolm Gladwell!"

Why Every Writer Should Master
The Art Of Languaging

All three of us Pirates write.

We do lots of other things, too. Pirate Christopher has two chart-topping podcasts, gives keynote speeches here and there, runs workshops with Silicon Valley venture capital firms, and advises start-ups on Category Design. Pirate Eddie advises Fortune 500 executives and venture capital and private equity backed category creators looking to go public on how to grow revenues and their valuations using Category Design principles. He also gives keynote speeches, and (on occasion) appears on CNBC to talk about company performance in the public markets. And Pirate Cole co-runs the largest digital writing cohort-based curriculum on the Internet, while ghostwriting for C-level executives, founders, and investors (while also writing his own books and viral Twitter threads).

But in addition to our entrepreneurial endeavors, we have used writing (and more importantly, languaging) to further separate ourselves from any and all comparison—and simultaneously clarify our own thinking. As a result, we have all become known for niches we own. Pirate Cole, the "digital writer;" Pirate Eddie, the "category guru to the Fortune 500;" Pirate Christopher, the "category design godfather to tech startups." Our individual success is not based exclusively on the quality of our work. Lots of people are "good" at the things we do.

We are successful because we are known for niches we own.

Our reputations are intertwined with our respective niches.

Languaging + Category Design = Legendary, Differentiated Career

Pirate Christopher has dyslexia. (And dyscalculia, and ADHD.)

When Pirate Eddie landed a column with HBR, his wife said, "How? You're a terrible writer!"

And Pirate Cole didn't know the difference between "your" and "you're" until he was almost 21 years old.

There are a lot of writers who are "better" than we are at writing. A lot.

Do you know their names?

Neither do we.

Another way of thinking about this would be: lots of writers are "better" than the 3 of us at different aspects of writing down words. But where else can you read about Languaging, and Superconsumers, and The Magic Triangle of Category Design? Our writing doesn't have to be "better." It illustrates different thinking, and it's not easily replaceable. That's why you value it, fellow Pirate. It was done on purpose. We didn't wait for the world to "discover" us. We didn't compare ourselves to business writers/thinkers of the past. We got busy evangelizing our "different." And when enough people "got" our point of view, our careers as writers/creators tipped. *ARRRRRRR!*

When you write, you are engaging in the process of clarifying your thinking. When you clarify your thinking, you have the opportunity to differentiate your thoughts from other unclarified thinkers and writers. When your thoughts become more and more differentiated than anything that currently exists, people listen. And when people listen, you become "the authority."

However, in order to become known for a niche you own (which is what separates the wealthy 1% of creators from the impoverished "creative middle class"), you must take this one step further and *invent new language to draw clear distinctions between what you're saying and what everyone else is saying.* When Pirate Christopher calls his podcast a "dialogue podcast," he is inventing language that separates what he does from what everyone else does (which is edit their podcasts and remove the little riffs and tangents that make dialogues authentic). Or when Pirate Cole calls himself a "digital writer," he is inventing language that separates how he approaches writing (using data gathered on social platforms) versus how "the old world" writes (alone, wearing a chapeau, smoking a corn cob pipe, staring out the window waiting for inspiration to strike). And when Pirate Eddie calls consumers who know your category better than anyone else and are willing to spend 30%-70% for your products/services "Superconsumers," that's languaging.

Like Malcolm Gladwell and "The Tipping Point," languaging is how you become known for a niche or an idea bigger than yourself.

Being A Skilled Writer Is Not The Same As Languaging

There is a difference between being a skilled writer and a writer who has the skill set of languaging.

We've met many skilled writers throughout our careers. They are incredible at what they do, and their talents are important. But that doesn't mean they are legendary at languaging (and is why many spend their whole careers earning a modest salary writing for a major publication or working at a marketing agency instead of becoming known for a niche they own, achieving financial freedom, and making a giant difference).

Furthermore, we know many excellent writers with far more impressive credentials than the three of us combined: PhDs in English/ Literature from Ivy League Schools, editors of top tier publications, and so on. These folks play an important role in helping currently established voices and entities tell their stories "better," but at the end of the day, they can't create content that stands alone (in the sense that if their entire livelihood was based upon customers paying for their words, they wouldn't be able to buy groceries or pay their rent). They help write books, but they don't write books themselves. They can critique, but they can't create. They don't change the course of the world.

This is because they have no point of view. They have nothing to say.

There are thousands of great writers. But there is only one "Tipping Point guy."

And while we're talking about writers, this applies to every type of creator and every type of company. Because every creator and every company is, and needs to be, a media company. A creator or a company without a media component today is like a creator or a company without a website. Part (if not all) of being a thought leader means "sharing your leading thoughts," aka your Point Of View, with the world—because the creator or company that sets the agenda in the space dominates the space.

How do you do that? With words.

And how do you distribute those words? By becoming a valuable "media company."

If you aren't earning 6 figures or more as a writer, you don't have a writing problem.

You have a languaging problem.

You could be the most talented writer on the planet, but if you are not strategically using language to change the way people think about and perceive who you are and what you write about, you are failing to draw a distinction between you and everyone else. Worse, you are probably doing the opposite of languaging, which means you are using unclarified, undifferentiated language and unconsciously inviting in comparison. You are telling the world you're "the same" as everyone else, which means you are easily replaceable. And anyone or anything that is easily replaceable is perceived to be "not rare" or "not valuable." A commodity.

Languaging & Category Design is about creating the opposite of a commodity.

To put a fine point on it: becoming known for a niche you own is not dependent upon you achieving anything externally. It's not about getting the blue checkmark on Twitter, or having a column with *The Atlantic*, or even becoming a *New York Times* best-selling author. **It's about inventing new language to represent new and differentiated ideas**, and educating people on the differences between what you're saying versus what has been said before (old vs new).

When you do this, and you refine and clarify your thinking (through writing) over the years, you "write the book" on the subject.

And he or she who writes the book on the subject is perceived to be the leader.

As Isaac Morehouse, CEO of Crash, puts it: "Be your own credential."

Why The Traditional Publishing World Is Dying—And Direct-To-Creator Is Thriving

The traditional publishing world played a mean trick on writers.

Over the past ten years, books (in every genre: health and wellness, psychology, relationships, life advice, but most especially, business) have gone from being "books" to glorified business cards. Writers have been taught (languaging used for evil, not good) that selling books is hard, readers don't buy books anymore, and it's far better to think of your book (or any of your intellectual property) as a means to an end: attracting clients, landing speaking gigs, "positioning yourself as a thought leader," and so on.

The myth here is: "You don't want the value of what you wrote. You want the value of the opportunities your writing *creates*."

But if selling books is so hard, and readers don't buy books anymore, then why does Penguin Random House publish 15,000 new titles every year? *Because these companies make money off the value of what you wrote—and the less you value it, the easier it is for them to acquire it from you.*

The single greatest misstep writers, authors, and business leaders make in the world of "content" is trading (or misvaluing) ownership over their scalable assets.

Writers think "books don't sell," and would rather take the perceived credibility of being published by a traditional publisher to warrant higher speaking and consulting fees.

But the truth is, it's the undifferentiated books that don't sell. *Differentiated books sell like hell!*

And if you have a differentiated book, and you knew it was differentiated, wouldn't you want to own 100% of it (just like a differentiated startup)?

Harry Potter would have sold millions of copies regardless of whether or not it was traditionally published—it was that "different." Same with word-of-mouth-wildfire books like *The Subtle Art of Not Giving A F*ck*, or *Atomic Habits*.

Were these authors still financially successful despite their deals with traditional publishers? Of course they were. A six-figure advance and making a million bucks in royalties is an amazingly rare outcome.

It just feels like peanuts when you know, while you made a million, your publisher made ten.

The direct-to-creator business model is (slowly) making writers realize their treasure chests have been getting looted.

For the first time in history, the digital revolution has created agency around ownership and monetization of content. Self-publishing on Amazon creates agency. Self-publishing on Substack creates agency. Launching a website in 15 minutes on Squarespace, uploading an eBook or PDF document for sale, and processing payments via Stripe creates agency.

Now, the myth writers got sold—"write a book, lose money, and you'll get more clients"—is proving false.

And the mega-category tailwind accelerating this shift is the move from Native Analog to Native Digital.

In a non-scalable, analog environment (the 1970s, 80s, and 90s, for example), an argument could be made for giving away your intellectual capital to get more analog work: consulting, speaking, and so on. But everyone in 2021 knows what you really want (the holy grail of 21st century "work") is to scale your digital business and shrink your analog business. Why would you trade valuable IP with a 99% profit margin and an increasing returns business model for an analog business that requires you to trade hours for dollars (regardless of the premium)?

In the same way Native Digitals (Millennials and Gen Zers) are 180 degrees different from Native Analogs (Baby Boomers and Gen Xers), the new model for becoming a legendary writer, creator, and even company is 180 degrees different from the old model. So much so, that writers who continue to associate themselves and their writing with old, analog platforms and business models (like writing for an undifferentiated publication like *Inc* or *Forbes*) now run the risk of damaging their digital reputations (Pirate Cole and Pirate Christopher both stopped writing for these types of undifferentiated publications a long time ago). In writing for these analog platforms, and adhering to business models that take advantage of the creator, you are (unconsciously) announcing your lack of differentiation to the world. Maybe more importantly, you're also announcing that you believe you need THEIR brand to build YOUR reputation.

Which, by definition, means you are not legendary (and bad at business).

"Eagles don't flock." —*Rick Bennett*

Now is the greatest time in history to be a writer.

Languaging in the context of Category Design combined with a direct-to-creator business model is how you build a legendary career.

Few writers think this way.

Instead, the vast majority want to feel "discovered" and validated by a 3rd-party publisher, magazine, company, or platform. They are willing to trade this feeling of acceptance for a) becoming known for a niche they own, b) having agency and freedom, and c) leveraging the new direct-to-creator business model and actually making money. They would rather have the blue checkmark of approval than have people actually listen to what they have to say and be financially rewarded for their ability to successfully do so.

This same phenomenon exists in the marketing world.

There are many ads and campaigns that win awards and receive prestigious recognition at fancy industry events and festivals (Cannes Lions, for example) that were not successful at making the cash register sing. For example, in 2011, Jell-O launched a campaign called "Pudding Face," created by *another-advertising-agency-named-after-its-founders* (Crispin Porter + Bogusky), complete with an interactive website & interactive billboard downtown New York City.

The idea of the campaign was to create a "Mood Meter" that measured how the world felt at any given moment based on the number of smiley and sad-face emojis posted on Twitter—the "Pudding Face" being updated in real time on the billboard. Jell-O would then tweet unhappy Twitter accounts with promotions to claim their free pudding (and turn that frown upside-down).

Was this campaign creative?

People in the world of advertising sure seemed to think so. "Pudding Face" led to a lot of back-patting when it first launched. And in

2012, when Saatchi & Saatchi hired away Brittany Poole, the copywriter behind the "Pudding Face" campaign, they touted her accomplishments in various press releases, emphasizing how lucky they were to have such a decorated copywriter joining their team. *In 2011, she won a Bronze Young Gun for her JELL-O Pudding Face Mood Meter campaign.*

The problem?

Jell-O's "Pudding Face" might have been "creative," but it didn't accomplish the goal of increasing sales. Instead, it scared children, and led to a sharp decline in sales. And less than three years later, CNBC reported the business had just seen a double-digit percentage drop in revenues.

Any awards Jell-O, Crispin Porter + Bogusky, or copywriters like Brittany Poole received from the campaign were just more examples of peers congratulating peers.

Awards are based on playing the "better" game.

When this becomes your measure for success, your entire headset is oriented toward impressing your colleagues and peers with your "better" work—which they judge.

Therefore, your self-worth (and your net worth) is 100% dependent upon your ability to receive their validation.

Legendary writers, creators, and entrepreneurs don't care about any of this.

What legendary writers, creators, and entrepreneurs care about is moving the world forward—regardless of whether or not they receive a pat on the back from their colleagues and the platforms responsible for handing out awards to those who "win." What they care about is making a difference. What they care about is having agency in their lives, and control over the profitability lever of their business.

All of which means, as a writer, if you value awards, titles, and recognition from your peers, then you value the "better" game. And if you value the "better" game, then you value being published by a traditional publishing company (books, magazines, digital publications, etc.) more than you value becoming known as unique and distinct, changing the world (however big or small), owning your intellectual property, and making money. Because if you valued any of those things, you wouldn't in a million years sell 90% ownership over your intellectual property to someone else. (Pirate Cole is the most successful writer to come out of his Alma mater by a wide margin, and yet the school refuses to acknowledge any of his accomplishments. Meanwhile, they love celebrating students who get short stories published in legacy magazines, or novels published by major publishing houses—even if it puts the writer in the poorhouse.)

So which do you value?

Getting prizes?

Or differentiating yourself and building a legendary business?

Differentiated Thinking + Languaging + Direct-To-Creator Business Model x A Growing Library Of Content = $$$$$$

Let's do some fun Pirate math and play the "which buried treasure is more valuable" game.

Let's say the three of us weren't Pirates, but folks pursuing prestige and credibility (as most who write and publish books with traditional publishing houses do). Conventional wisdom here is to write a book proposal (in private—*don't you dare share your ideas with anyone, you mercenary, lest they might steal them!*), work with an agent, and sell your manuscript-in-progress to a traditional publisher. Industry standard deal terms here are an advance plus 5-15% royalties after the advance has been paid out (said differently: you are selling 90% ownership in your product in exchange for the money they give you upfront). And industry average advances for first-time authors range from $5,000 (or sometimes $0.00) on the low end to $50,000 on the higher end. Six-figure advances are few and far between, and seven-figure advances are reserved for celebrities and social media stars with huge audiences (and the fact these individuals take these deals is a clear sign they're paying "The Better Game," since they're the last people who need help with distribution).

These non-Pirate authors would have to sell ~30,000 copies of their book at $17 per book to "earn out" their $50,000 advance and start receiving royalties.

For context, this is *ten times* the industry average. Most traditionally published books only sell ~3,000 copies.

At this point in the conversation, everyone always says the same thing.

"But publishers help with distribution!"

No, they don't. They help the top 1% of their authors with distribution (and, for context, Penguin Random house publishes over 70,000 digital and 15,000 print books each year—they proudly proclaim their strained resources on their website). For everyone else, they give a $5,000 to $50,000 advance in exchange for 90% ownership and then *expect you to use your advance to market the product you no longer own.*

But for argument's sake, let's assume they do help with distribution, and they hit "upload" on Amazon for you. (An intern somewhere is very proud of the contribution they've made toward the success of your work.) Now, because your royalty split is only 10%, you need to sell 10x more copies in order to make the same amount of money.

You "get more distribution," but your path to profitability just got exponentially harder.

So the question becomes: which obstacle do you want to face? Having more distribution, but needing to sell 10x more copies to turn a profit? Or "not having as much distribution," but needing to sell a fraction of the copies (online) to earn the same amount of money?

For what it's worth: how publishers get you into bookstores is by calling them up and asking them to carry your book. And what causes the bookstore to carry your book is *how well your book is selling, or is projected to sell.* So if bookstores really mean that much to you, or you firmly believe bookstores are what propel sales (what generation are you living in?), you can call them up yourself. You can also upload a copy of your book to IngramSpark, and bookstores can order copies to carry.

Now let's say you are a Pirate! (ARRRRRRRRR!)

Instead of giving up 90% ownership for a paltry advance, you leverage the direct-to-creator business model.

You've been writing for a while now. You've clarified and differentiated your thinking. You've used languaging to draw further distinction between what you're saying that's new versus what has been said before and is old. And now, you want to be in the business of owning that intellectual property as it spreads across the Internet.

Any copies you sell on your own, or on your website, you earn 100% of the profits. But let's say the majority of the sales come from a platform like Amazon, which takes 30% of the transaction. To be clear: Amazon does not own your content. You're free to do with it whatever you please elsewhere on the Internet, and can continue to monetize it over and over again. The 30% take is purely a middle-man fee for processing the transaction on their platform. Assuming you sell the *same amount of copies* as you did with a traditional publisher (30,000 copies at $17 per book), this would generate total revenues of $500,000.

That's 7x more than if you sold your IP to a traditional publisher. (Who, by the way, is going to do the same exact thing: take your ebook/book file and upload it to Amazon for you.)

Now, let's take this a step further.

When you're a Pirate operating with a direct-to-creator business model, this means you can do whatever you want with your content. You can chop it up, slice it and dice it, and most importantly, *monetize it dozens of* *different ways **and multiple times in the future.***

- Content can be sold via newsletter.
- Content can be republished behind Medium's paywall.
- Content can be combined and sold as an ebook/book.
- Content can be stripped apart and sold as stand-alone downloads.
- Content can become podcasts.
- Content can become the foundation of curriculums, courses, communities, and more.

For example, Pirate Cole has been republishing his entire library of articles behind Medium's paywall for more than 2 years—and has made more than $100,000 doing so. This means he is collecting royalties on intellectual property he wrote historically. And as more social publishing platforms launch their own direct-to-creator models, he will be able to do the same thing again and again. (Because he owns the content!)

So now let's assume, as a Pirate, you decide to flip the publishing model on its head.

Instead of writing a book, first, you decide to create shorter-form content and distribute it via paid newsletter (on a platform like Substack). This allows you to:

- Tighten your audience feedback loop and refine your content & thinking as you go
- Build your audience along the way versus in the 11th hour right before your book comes out
- Maintain 100% ownership over the content
- And start generating revenue on day one.

Said differently: instead of trading 90% ownership of your content for an advance that buys you six months or a year of time to write your book and then having to use your advance to fast-track your audience building and marketing, you can maintain 100% ownership and generate *the same or more* as your advance would have paid you, while refining your content and building your audience along the way.

ARRRRRRRRR!

Now let's take Pirate Eddie's Superconsumer math and say that the Top 10% of your customers generate 70% of the sales. This rings true, as the vast majority of our own books were big bulk orders by the top venture capital firms, Fortune 500 companies, and large conferences (if you want to know how *New York Times* best-sellers juice the rankings, this is how they do it). In other cases, Superconsumers repeatedly buy the same book over and over again as gifts. (Think about how many times you've bought the same book—for yourself, for friends and family, etc.)

Of the 30,000 books you sell, we can assume 21,000 (70% of sales) are bought by the top 10% of your consumers—your Superconsumers. To keep the math simple, let's say that each Super bought 21 copies for themselves, their companies, and as Christmas and birthday gifts for their friends and family members. That is 1,000 Superconsumers. And since a Superconsumer of 1 category is a super of 9 other categories, we can also assume the 1,000 Supers who bought your book are also subscribing members of your paid newsletter.

At $200 per year for your paid content, that's another $200,000 in annual revenue *that you get paid to write your next book* (because newsletter content can become book content).

Ba-da-bing, ba-da-boom.

Through this new category lens, each book is a breakthrough product innovation (you are creating it with your audience versus by yourself in your apartment with no feedback loop), written with a breakthrough business model (paid newsletter), that creates a breakthrough data flywheel (your email list).

You're just successfully prosecuted The Magic Triangle as a writer.

And while you might not be on the path to getting prizes and awards from industry peers, you're now on the path to success as you define it, financial freedom, creative autonomy, and complete control over your future.

CHAPTER SEVEN

Becoming A Top 444 Author

How To Turn Your Breakthrough
Ideas Into A Best-Selling Book
(According To The World's First
Non-Fiction Study)

Whether you are an Obvious or Non-Obvious writer, creator, entrepreneur, or executive, the pinnacle of sharing your insights with the world is writing a book.

All three of us have written books (individually first, and then collectively), and despite achieving success in other areas of life, there is a remarkable difference in the way people's eyes light up when they discover each of us is an "author." Pirate Christopher has two #1 ranking business podcasts and when he tells people he is a podcaster, they sort of shrug and say, "That's cool," *because hey, anyone with a smartphone and an internet connection can start a podcast.* But when he tells people he is an author, their focus narrows and their voice gets quiet and the whole color of the room changes. Hence why so many people, whether they actually enjoy writing or not (or have anything valuable to say) want to publish a book at some point in their lives.

Saying you are an author is special.

Now, obviously we are not here to tell people how to crap out 200 pages of platitudes, slap a cover on it, and give themselves a new badge ("author") to wear at tomorrow's dinner party. Writing a book for the sake of writing a book is a waste of your time, and the reader's.

Instead, if you want to make a difference in the world (first) and you want the best possible shot at producing a best-selling book, we want to give you a framework for turning your Obvious and/or Non-Obvious insights, perspectives, and stories into an asset that not only gives you the title of "author," but changes the way people think AND pays you dividends long into the future.

How did we come up with this framework?

By analyzing the top 444 best-selling business books in the last two decades.

It is important for you to know that most people in the idea / creation / innovation / writing business will never consume the game-changing insights you are about to read. Of the few who do consume this, even fewer will internalize and take action on these insights. That creates a massive advantage for you.

A Category Science Study Of How Ideas Scale

If you have no ambitions of being a writer or author, you may feel the impulse to dismiss what we're about to share with you.

Here's why we would encourage you not to.

No matter what career path you choose, or what industry you're in, or what role you command (whether you're an intern or a C-level executive), the trajectory of your professional life is a direct reflection of the quality of your ideas. Intellectual capital. And the lens most people use for evaluating ideas is the same lens they use for naming their cat.

"Do I like this? Or do I not like this?"

And this is 100% appropriate for naming your cat. However, if you want to make a difference and share ideas with the world that have a transformative effect (communicated in book form or not), using the same lens you use to name your cat is unproductive. (And we have sat in *a lot* of rooms with a lot of "smart people" who suddenly forget how to be smart and decide to evaluate the company's category, POV, messaging, and that quarter's creative campaign through the lens of: "Do I like this? Or do I not like this?")

But coming up with unique, compelling, understandable ideas is only 50% of the game.

The other 50% (which almost never gets talked about) is how to come up with **ideas that scale**. Because, as it turns out, a brilliant idea that never gets talked about, shared, and implemented isn't actually "a great idea." (If a drunken Pirate falls overboard at sea, does he make a sound?) Meanwhile, a not-so-great idea that successfully captures the imagination of modern society has the power to change the world.

Whether we like it or not, we are all in the "scaling ideas" business.

Unfortunately, while a ton of information exists on how to come up with great ideas, very little information exists on how to come up with *ideas that scale.*

Ask Malcolm Gladwell what makes him Malcolm Gladwell, the best-selling author who has sold millions of copies of unique, differentiated thinking, and he can't tell you. Don't believe us? Watch his

MasterClass, or James Patterson's, or Dan Brown's, or Judy Bloom's (all writers and thinkers we deeply respect), and what you'll walk away with are a few tactical golden nuggets: "Write for the reader and don't be afraid to leave them hanging." But ask these authors what makes one of their ideas (books) more successful than the others, ask them **what caused some of their ideas to scale**, and they all repeat the same answers:

- "The world was ready for something like this."
- "I guess it was just a better story."
- "We did a lot of marketing for that one."
- "I suppose it connected with the reader."
- "I poured my heart and soul into that book."

These answers are mildly inspirational at best and unconsciously misleading at worst. They may provide relief during a Q&A in an auditorium, but they do not shed any analytical insight into why certain ideas scale and others go nowhere. Furthermore, isn't it interesting that some of the most successful writers and thinkers in society struggle to engineer serendipity twice? They write a best-selling book sharing a breakthrough idea, only for their follow-up book(s) to fall flat. Why is that?

Because nobody really knows why some ideas scale and others don't. Not the authors, not the editors, and certainly not the publishers.

Until now.

Like a lot of the things we write, what we are about to share with you operates on multiple planes of thinking at the same time. This is the most extensive research done on **why certain ideas scale and others do not,** leveraging modern business data through a Category Science lens. If you want to understand how to create a different future for your readers, customers, and/or clients, you need to understand how those new and different futures must be presented in order to maximize scalability and impact. Otherwise, you will waste years of work (leading up to the launch and after the launch) and tremendous resources trying to scale an idea that is very likely flawed at its root.

Books are the most professional and powerful way to present new ideas through a point of view. And why we were fascinated studying the best-selling business books of the past 20 years is not solely because we wanted to create a framework for engineering success ourselves. We also wanted to objectively understand how new category POVs succeed or fail based on how that POV gets presented and who the presenter is. And what we learned is that a breakthrough idea communicated by the wrong person doesn't scale. And neither does a conventional idea by someone with all the credibility in the world. Analyzing the sales data of the Top 444 best-selling business books of the past 20 years is emblematic of what breakthrough POVs scale and do not.

And why.

The First Breakthrough Study: Analyzing The Top 444 Best-Selling Business Books Of The Past Two Decades

A little backstory:

The three of us are "driven achievers." Meaning no matter what it is we do, it is crucial to us (like breathing) that our actions accomplish three goals:

- Our work helps other people, and produces legendary outcomes for those we reach.
- Our work is radically different, and impossible to substitute with a "next-best alternative."
- Our work is profitable, rapidly growing, and capable of unlocking life-changing outcomes for ourselves and our

families.

When the three of us first met, we connected over a shared desire to help entrepreneurs, executives, marketers, thinkers, creators, and writers create new categories, exit "The Better Trap," and build businesses that created new and different futures for humanity. We were tired of hearing intelligent people give unintelligent advice, and share business and marketing "thinking" we knew (from years of experience) to be wrong. And not just wrong, but dangerously unproductive. Category Pirates became our vehicle to educate those who were willing to "think different" a new lens through which to see the world and produce legendary results).

Of course, as driven achievers, this was only the beginning.

The more time we spent together, the more "mini-books" we wrote and published, and the more Pirates who hopped aboard this Pirate Ship, the more we realized the opportunity in front of us: to be the first "writing band" to produce decades of work—together. And not just meaningful work, but best-selling work. We have one volume setting, and it's 11. So about a year into writing together, we set our first big, hairy, audacious goal: to write a business book that sells over 1,000,000 copies.

Maybe it will be this book you are reading right now. Or our next book, *Intellectual Capitalist*. Or one of our many books after that.

The point is: we don't know when we will reach that first island. All we know is that if we keep sailing in this direction, we will. But to improve our odds of success (the last thing we want is to die from dysentery while out at sea), we thought it would be a good idea to study the best-selling business books before us and see if we could spot any recurring themes and create a repeatable model for producing best-selling books.

And what we discovered was a goldmine of insights.

The Study (Category Science)

To get our hands on a reliable data set, we partnered with NPD

BookScan, the "gold standard" in tracking sales data in the publishing market. We sourced the top 500 best-selling business books from the past 20 years (some books had duplicate best-sellers due to varying formats: paperback, hardcover, eBook, etc., bringing the total down to 444). The data covers all measured "consumer" channels (Amazon, Barnes & Noble, and other retail outlets where consumers shop for books), and it excludes "business to business" sales (like a large purchase by a single corporation or by one conference for a speech) and resale data.

Once we received the data, we started by tagging the books with dozens of different variables to see if we noticed any high-level trends:

- Publication date
- Average number of pages
- Week 1 sales
- Month 1 sales
- Year 1 sales
- Year 3 sales
- Year 5 sales
- Year 10 sales
- Category
- Number of Amazon reviews
- Reviews per book per author
- Book revenue
- Author 20-year revenue

And dozens more...

The big question we were trying to answer was: *"What makes some writers stand the test of time, and others hit the New York Times bestseller list and then fizzle out months (or weeks, or even days) later?"* If we were going to commit to spending the next 10, 20, 30+ years writing legendary business "thinking" mini-books and big-books, how could we maximize our contribution with our limited time here on earth? What causes a book to make a difference (to "scale") for a moment versus a book that makes a difference for years, decades, or centuries? And how could we create a new framework *based on data* for ourselves so that everything we write, every idea we come up with, has the highest percentage chance of "scaling" and reaching readers all over the world?

What Business Book Publishers Do Not Know, Wish They Knew, And Don't Want You To Know

The entire reason writers sign with traditional publishers is because they think the publisher knows something they don't (they have "the secret recipe").

What this study (shockingly) revealed to us is that the publishing world, as well as the business world at large, doesn't know the first thing about writing books that make a giant difference (and before completing this study, neither did we—despite the fact that we've sold hundreds of thousands of books in the past). In fact, just about everything we have written up until this point is riddled with "mistakes" through this new lens and framework. Even the major publishers (we've been published by a few) don't know what separates a book that sells a million copies from a book that sells 10,000 copies (and they certainly don't have a reliable framework for engineering serendipity twice).

Which is why we are so excited to share it with you.

Here's what we found:

Note: These insights, and this new framework, applies to all non-fiction books in just about every subcategory imaginable. For the sake of focus however, we are not including fiction at all here. That's not to say there aren't applicable takeaways that can be applied to fiction, we just want to be clear that our study did not include any fiction titles.

The 7 Best-Selling Business Book Categories

Before you set out to write a best-selling book (or a viral blog post, or a newsworthy press release, or any other kind of asset that you want to have a giant impact), it's worth considering whether the topic you are excited to pursue has any "scaling potential."

Now, we want to be very clear about something: not every book or idea needs to be a grand-slam sales home run. There is absolutely something to be said for writing a niche book (especially if you self-publish it and reap 100% of the financial upside). For example: Pirate Cole's book, *The Art & Business of Online Writing*, is a niche, self-published book for digital writers. It has sold a little over 10,000 copies (at the time of our writing this) after being in the market for about 2 years, and continues to generate roughly $2,500 in sales income per month, every month.

However, that book has been very effective at amplifying Pirate Cole's position as the Category King of the "Digital Writing" category, as well as opened doors for other lucrative business ventures and opportunities—such as attracting high-paying ghostwriting clients and startups looking for help with their Category Languaging.

Writing a niche book can be a great first step to your path of becoming a successful writer, creator, entrepreneur, and industry thought leader.

Just don't be surprised when it fails to scale.

But if you want to swing for the fences, then your big idea needs to fall into one of these 7 categories:

- Personal Development
- Personal Finance
- Insights/Thinking

- Leadership
- Case Study/Allegory
- Functional Excellence
- Relationships

Almost all of the Top 444 best-selling business books of the past 20 years can be organized into these 7 buckets. **This is not an accident.** As Pirate Cole says often: "The size of the question dictates the size of the audience." Which means in order to reach millions of readers, or write a book that unlocks millions of dollars in revenue, you need to answer big, universal questions. If you don't, it doesn't matter how "good" you think the book is—the question the book is answering doesn't have enough scale.

Now, these 7 mega-categories are not all equal.

Some are much larger than others, and some inherently sell more copies over longer time horizons (versus becoming a best-seller for a year and then sales falling off a cliff).

So let's break each one down.

Personal Development

The Personal Development category of business books is the largest and most profitable category.

Of the 444 top selling business books since 2004, it makes up 23% of the titles, 25% of Amazon reviews, 28% of unit volume sold, and 31% of revenue. Personal Development captures ~35% more of its fair share of revenue in the business book category (31% of revenue divided by 23% of book titles) and has +3% higher share of revenue vs. share of units—making it the most productive and most profitable unit economics of any category of business book.

Fair share is important because each book takes up roughly the same amount of real estate— both in a store or on a webpage. Personal Development books generate 35% more revenue while using the same amount of analog or digital real estate as an average business book. Retailers love this and will keep it on their shelves longer. Personal Development is roughly 11% higher price per unit vs. the unit economics of an average business book. Unit economics are important as books with higher pricing generate more for the retailer, the publisher, and of course the author.

Personal Development books also have the most staying power. We organized the data set into Year 1, Year 2, Year X sales regardless of publish date (since 2004), and what we found is that Personal Development is the only category of business book with an aggregate CAGR (compound annual growth rate) consistently positive from 3-year CAGR to 15-year CAGR.

Said simply: these books start strong and stay strong.

Book examples:

- *The Difference Maker: Making Your Attitude Your Greatest Asset*
- *Talent Is Overrated: What Really Separates World-Class Performers From Everybody Else*
- *Find Your Why: A Practical Guide For Discovering Purpose For You and Your Team*
- *The 7 Habits of Highly Effective People*
- *The 8th Habit: From Effectiveness To Greatness*

Personal Development is the largest category in the book publishing space. (Which is a massive achievement considering the Personal Development category sat on the fringes of society for a long time. Pirate Christopher remembers taking his first Personal Development course in 1987. Some people thought he had joined a cult, while others were made upset even hearing the then-radical-idea of "self improvement.")

If your goal is to write a book that sells more than 1,000,000 copies (or scale any idea into the mainstream conversation), your best shot is to write that book in a way that is related to personal development or life advice. Go peruse the *New York Times* best-seller list and you'll notice the vast majority of the books fall into the Personal Development category.

Now, here's the nuance:

While *technically* any book category can in some way be related to Personal Development, there is a giant sales and impact difference between Personal Development books about an idea versus Personal Development books that speak directly "to" the reader. What our study revealed was that the best-selling business books of the past 20 years almost always addressed the reader directly:

- "Here's how YOU can..."
- "Here's why YOU should..."
- "Here's what YOU need to know..."

Through this lens, we could spot quite a few business books where this was the intention, but fell short because the book was more about the author's story or a company's story opposed to the reader's story. **This is a very subtle but important point.** Even if you want to share your own stories and experiences, there's a difference between writing a book where your story is the "main character" and the reader has to extract their own takeaways versus a book where the reader is the "main character" and your stories are examples that reinforce the advice you are providing.

Said differently: if you want to write a best-selling book, the reader needs to understand how and why it's going to help them directly. Books about "interesting topics" that don't give the reader anything immediately actionable to their own lives fall flat.

Personal Finance

Personal Finance represents 25% of titles, 31% of Amazon reviews, but only 23% of unit volume and 19% of revenue.

While Personal Finance is the second-largest percent of revenue at 19%, **it is 24% less productive and 18% less profitable than the average business book.** (Go figure!.... Books about money make less money.)

This either means Personal Finance books are priced lower to start, or are discounted more aggressively as their sales fail to reach expectations.

In addition, Personal Finance books have much less staying power than Personal Development books, with positive CAGR sales in early years (3 and 5-year CAGR), but then going negative from 6 to 11-year CAGR and eventually staying flat around 12 to 15-year CAGR.

Book Examples:

- Rich Dad, Poor Dad: What The Rich Teach Their Kids About Money—That The Poor And The Middle Class Do Not!
- Rich Woman: A Book On Investing For Women— Because I Hate Being Told What to Do
- Broke Millennial: Stop Scraping By And Get Your Financial Life Together
- The Automatic Millionaire Homeowner: A Powerful Plan To Finish Rich In Real Estate
- Missed Fortune 101: A Starter Kit To Becoming a Millionaire

As the next-largest category, Personal Finance shares many similar themes with Personal Development.

- **Personal Development:** "Here's how YOU can change your life."
- **Personal Finance:** "Here's how YOU can get rich."

Notice again the importance of the book speaking directly to the reader: in the title, subtitle, and all throughout the book as well.

Insights/Thinking

Insights/Thinking is the third-largest revenue book category making up 15% of titles, 12% of reviews, 15% of unit volume, and 16% of revenue. This tells us it has about average productivity and average unit economics.

What is interesting is its staying power. Insights/Thinking books have a flat 3-year CAGR, but are positive from 4 year to 15-year CAGRs. These books start out slower, but generate steady sales after that.

Book Examples:

- *The Innovator's Dilemma: The Revolutionary Book That Will Change the Way You Do Business*
- *Crossing the Chasm: Marketing And Selling Disruptive Products To Mainstream Customers*
- *Purple Cow: Transform Your Business By Being Remarkable*
- *The Daily Drucker: 366 Days of Insight And Motivation For Getting the Right Things Done*
- *The Fifth Discipline: The Art & Practice Of The Learning Organization*

Insights/Thinking is significantly smaller than Personal Development and Personal Finance. However, it's where radically different thinkers usually find themselves in the bookstore. (This is our favorite category—for good and bad.)

The key here is, when writing an Insights/Thinking book, to try to make it as Personal Development focused as possible. Insights/Thinking books that are interesting but not actionable rarely reach the heights of a "this book changed the way I thought about my life." A simple example would be Malcolm Gladwell's *Outliers* vs Mark Manson's *The Subtle Art of Not Giving a F*ck*. *Outliers* is a fascinating book, but it's more interesting than it is actionable. As a result, you finish reading it, maybe repeat one of the interesting takeaways at a dinner party, and then that's about it. Whereas *The Subtle Art of Not Giving a F*ck*, although less interesting, feels 10x more actionable to the reader: "Here's how I can stop giving a fuck, too."

And for context: *The Subtle Art* has outsold *Outliers* by a factor of five, in half the time.

So, when writing an Insights/Thinking book, don't fall into the trap of thinking "I need to show people how smart of a thought leader I am." Use your deep insights & new thinking to speak directly to the reader's wants, needs, hopes, dreams, desires, and aspirations in life.

Leadership

The fourth-largest revenue category is Leadership, making up 13% of titles, 11% of Amazon reviews, 14% of unit volume, and 15% of revenue.

This tells us Leadership books are reasonably more productive (15%) and have slightly higher unit economics (7%). Leadership books also have moderate staying power with positive 3 and 10-year CAGR, before going negative around 11 to 15-year CAGR.

Book Examples:

- The New Gold Standard: 5 Leadership Principles For Creating A Legendary Customer Experience Courtesy Of The Ritz-Carlton Hotel Company
- Leadershift: The 11 Essential Changes Every Leader Must Embrace
- The Mentor Leader: Secrets To Building People And Teams That Win Consistently
- Multipliers: How The Best Leaders Make Everyone Smarter
- The 5 Levels of Leadership: Proven Steps To Maximize Your Potential

Again, actionable Leadership books that speak directly to the reader ("How YOU can become a legendary leader...") tend to outperform "interesting" Leadership books about the subject itself. The other nuance here is that the best-selling Leadership books tend to come from well-known leaders. (Nobody wants to learn how to become a legendary leader from some random guy or gal, no matter how well-written the book is). For example: a reader is far more likely to buy Phil Jackson's book on leadership than a book from some no-name entrepreneur who, although successful in his or her own right, does not immediately seem like "the most interesting or credible" source of information.

We notice a lot of business leaders tend to want to write leadership books (because they seem like "what sells"), when in reality, these writers and thought leaders are better off writing a Personal Development, Personal Finance, or Insights/Thinking book instead—if they want their ideas to scale.

Case Study/Allegory

Case Study/Allegory is the third-smallest revenue category, making up 11% of titles, 11% of Amazon reviews, 10% of unit volume, and 9% of revenue. It also has slightly lower productivity and pricing power than the average top 444 business book.

From a sales longevity standpoint, Case Study/Allegory books are the opposite of Insights/Thinking. They start out okay at the 3-year CAGR, but have consistently negative CAGRs from 4 year sales and beyond.

And here's why:

Case Study/Allegory books only remain relevant as long as the stories they are curating remain relevant.

Book Examples:

- *Onward: How Starbucks Fought For Its Life Without Losing Its Soul*

- *Getting Naked: A Business Fable About Shedding The Three Fears That Sabotage Client Loyalty*
- *Too Big to Fail: The Inside Story Of How Wall Street And Washington Fought To Save The Financial System—And Themselves*
- *The Hard Thing About Hard Things: Building A Business When There Are No Easy Answers*
- *Fast Food Nation: The Dark Side Of The All-American Meal*

For example: does anyone today want to read a business book from the 1990s about the success of Blockbuster? Of course not. Because time went by and we all saw how that story ended: Blockbuster got clobbered and Netflix stole the show. And while it might seem like a great idea to write a book about Netflix today, it's worth considering whether the Netflix story (like Blockbuster) will still be relevant 10 or 20 years from now.

The Case Study/Allegory category is the clearest example from our study of what happens to long-term book sales when you write about something with a limited shelf life. People are going to want to read about how to be happy or disciplined or confident (Personal Development) until the end of time. People are going to want to read about the timeless principles of how to get rich (Personal Finance) forever. But people will only want to read case studies and stories about other people, companies, and industries as long as those people, companies, and industries remain relevant.

Functional Excellence

Functional Excellence is about how to do something (a skill). And here, like the Case Study/Allegory category, time horizons are limited.

For example, today:

- Do you want to read a book today about how to build an audience on Myspace?

- Do you want to read a book about how to change the axle on your horse-drawn carriage?
- Do you want to read a book about how to change the settings on your Nokia flip phone?

Of course not. All of those skills were relevant in the past, and are no longer relevant today.

Functional Excellence is the second-smallest book category, making up 8% of titles, 7% of Amazon reviews, 6% of unit volume, and 6% of revenue.

It has lesser productivity and unit economics, relatively speaking.

And while sales over time remain consistent from 3 year to 8-year CAGR, they fall off a cliff after that.

Pirate Eddie was very disappointed to see this analysis and realize his book, *Superconsumers* (about pinpointing the most profitable, prescient, and powerful consumers in a category) fell into one of the weakest categories of business books. And *Superconsumers* was published by Harvard Business Review Press. (Guess they didn't know it either!) *Superconsumers* would have been much more successful (would have "scaled") if it had been written more as a Personal Development, Personal Finance, or Insights/Thinking book—not a Functional Excellence book. (The book's subtitle is a dead giveaway: *A Simple, Speedy, and Sustainable Path to Superior Growth.* This has Functional Excellence written all over it.)

Book Examples:

- Profit First: Transform Your Business From A Cash-Eating Monster To A Money-Making Machine
- Building A Storybrand: Clarify Your Message So Customers Will Listen
- *The Lean Six Sigma Pocket Toolbook: A Quick Reference Guide To Nearly 100 Tools For Improving Quality And Speed*

- *Never Split The Difference: Negotiating As If Your Life Depended On It*
- *Little Red Book Of Selling: 12.5 Principles Of Sales Greatness: How to Make Sales Forever*

Functional Excellence books are the easiest to write in the present moment (they are essentially How To Guides), but the shelf life of the book is 100% dependent upon the relevance of that skill to society. It's very common to see writers and thinkers race to write "The Ultimate Guide" of a new, emerging industry, only for those books to pop, grab short-term attention, and then become replaced by "The Ultimate Guide Revised" a few years later—putting that writer, creator, or industry thought leader on a hamster wheel of always needing to create the next-new How To guide opposed to building a library of timeless Personal Development, Personal Finance, or Insights/Thinking content that gets more valuable over time—not less. (*Think and Grow Rich* sells more copies today than it did when it was first published in 1937!)

Even worse, in some cases, the writer gets deeply associated with the category (say "stereo installation") and when the category becomes devalued by a new, emerging new category (say "smart home stereo setup") the Functional Excellence "guru" gets repositioned as an out-of-trend dinosaur.

So, if you are going to write a Functional Excellence book, realize you are optimizing for the short-term (which is fine) and let go of any exceptions of being paid long-term dividends for your work today. Furthermore, if you are going to stay on the hamster wheel of creating more new Functional Excellence material, be sure to lean aggressively into the future—otherwise you run the risk of creating new Functional Excellence material in a shrinking category.

Relationships

This is the smallest book category, making up 5% of titles, 4% of

Amazon reviews, 5% of unit volume, and 5% of book revenue.
Relationships as a category have average productivity, and average profitability growth until about the 7 year mark—when growth picks up.

Book Examples:

- Dare To Lead: Brave Work. Tough Conversations. Whole Hearts
- The 5 Languages of Appreciation In the Workplace: Empowering Organizations By Encouraging People
- The Hard Hat: 21 Ways To Be A Great Teammate
- Necessary Endings: The Employees, Businesses, And Relationships That All of Us Have to Give Up In Order to Move Forward
- The Little Black Book Of Connections: 6.5 Assets For Networking Your Way To Rich Relationships

Despite being one of the largest topic categories in the publishing industry, the success of Relationships books depends heavily on whether the book leans Personal Development/Personal Finance/Leadership, or leans more towards Insights/Thinking, Case Study/Allegory, or Functional Excellence.

For example, notice the perceived shelf life of these different (made up) Relationships books depending on which "bucket" the book falls into:

- [**Personal Development**]: How To Stay Happily Married If You Are Married To Your Co-Founder
- [**Personal Finance**]: How Co-Founders Who Are Married Can Maximize Their Taxes And Make More Money Together
- [**Leadership**]: How To Lead A Company If Your Co-Founder Is Your Husband
- [**Insights/Thinking**]: How Meditation Can Heal Relationships Between Life Partners Who Are Also Business Partners

- [Case Study/Allegory]: How Beyoncé And Jay-Z Became
  A Power Couple In Business And In Life
- [Functional Excellence]: How To Get More Twitch Sub-
  scribers By Playing Video Games With Your Wife

Even if the content is largely the same, the perception of the book's relevance to the reader AND the book's relevance over time changes drastically depending on what category of book it is. (The category always makes the brand.)

Which is why, before you even sit down to start writing, it's worth considering what type of book you want to write—and whether that type of book has the potential to achieve the goal you desire for yourself. Every writer says, "I want to write a best-seller." But does your book have the best-selling components? If not, no amount of marketing is going to make your dream come true.

Idea vs Author: Is The Reader Buying Your Idea? Or Is The Reader Buying "You?"

The next big part of our study was looking at the differences between book covers that were Idea-Centric versus Author-Centric.

- **Idea-Centric:** The book's title, subtitle, cover image, and content is about educating readers on a new & different idea.
- **Author-Centric:** The book's title, subtitle, cover image, and content is about educating readers on a familiar idea based on the author's credibility/celebrity.

Idea-Centric books have slightly better unit economics generating slightly more revenue per unit, whereas Author-Centric books generate more Amazon reviews, but slightly less revenue per unit. They also have the best staying power with 3-year CAGRs that are flat, but steadily grow over time thereafter. Whereas Author-Centric books start out strong at 3-4 year CAGRs, but go negative after that.

What this data underscores are Category Design's core principles proven out in book sales.

When the idea is about a problem or opportunity (category) for the reader/customer/subscriber/user, the likelihood of attracting new readers goes up. But when the idea is about the author (brand), the likelihood of attracting new readers goes down. Said differently: the degree to which people care about the author is a function of how much they care about the ideas that author, thinker, or thought leader is communicating in the world. The category makes the brand—not the other way around.

Digging deeper, we do see interesting nuances when you blend both data sets together.

Idea-Centric books and book covers generate superior unit economics inside the Personal Development and Insights/Thinking categories. (So if you are going to write a Personal Development or Insights/Thinking book, *you can't make it about yourself.* If you do, you are squandering the biggest opportunity you have to "scale" your ideas—which is to make it directly applicable and actionable to the reader.)

Combine Personal Development and Insights/Thinking books with Idea-Centric Covers

Personal Development books do better when paired with an Idea-Centric cover, but under-perform with an Author-Centric cover. Again, this is because Personal Development books are about the reader, not the author! (This runs counter to the "Personal Branding" BS in the world that preaches to "share your story." The data shows no one cares about your story—unless it is directly applicable to them.)

The same is true of Insights/Thinking books since the category is about the ideas, not the author.

The categories where Author-Centric books and book covers yield better results are in Personal Finance, Leadership, Case Study/Allegory, and Functional Excellence. This makes logical sense.

- You want to learn Personal Finance from someone who is rich.
- You want to learn Leadership from someone who is a legendary leader.
- You want to read about Case Studies from someone with inside knowledge, or someone who has done a tremendous amount of research.
- You want to acquire Functional Excellence from someone who is a master of their domain.

So, if you are writing books (or scaling ideas) in any of these 4 categories, you're incentivized to lean on your personal credibility. And if you don't have a strong sense of personal credibility, you shouldn't be writing a book or scaling an idea in one of these 4 categories. You should be venturing into the Personal Development or Insights/Thinking categories.

How To Ascend Up The 7 Best-Selling Categories

What's the takeaway from all this data?

The way you increase the likelihood of your idea "scaling," as well as the likelihood of writing a best-selling book is by ascending up these 7 categories. Because the higher you ascend up these categories, the more timeless the material becomes and the more pricing power you have.

For example:

- Instead of writing a Personal Finance book (or worse, a Personal Finance book that leans on timely Case Studies and/or Functional Excellence advice), you should strive to write a Personal Finance book that leans Insights/Thinking or Personal Development.

- Instead of writing a Case Study/Allegory or Functional Excellence book, you should strive to use the underlying takeaways from those case studies and the timeless wisdom from your functional excellence to write a Leadership, Insights/Thinking, or Personal Development book.

- And even if you are going to write an Insights/Thinking book, you should avoid the trap of writing an "interesting" book and instead leverage your new insights and different thinking to write an "actionable" Personal Development book.

In short: all roads lead to the two largest categories with the most pricing power, which are Insights/Thinking and Personal Development.

So You Want To Write A Book: Business Thought Leader Hypothetical Scenario

Now let's put these insights into practice. (ARRRRRRR!!!!!)

Scenario A: No-Name CEO/Thought Leader

Let's say you are the CEO of a successful company (or maybe you're a professor, executive, leader, creator, or anyone else who wants to make the future different), and you want to write a book. Publicly traded or venture-backed startup, $1M or $1B or $100B in revenue, it doesn't matter. You're the CEO of a company a small group of people know and recognize, and the rest of the world has never heard of. That doesn't mean you aren't successful! Let's just be honest about where you are starting from—so that you can choose the right category and maximize your chances for writing a bestseller. (All three of us started at the bottom as authors.)

Conventional wisdom (particularly from a traditional publisher) would be for you to write a Leadership book. Leadership sells, right? Well, we would encourage you *not* to.

ur analysis shows that Leadership works better for Author-Centric ideas—and in order for you to write an Author-Centric book, you need to be someone the world and/or your industry recognizes (your reputation in this category really matters). And since you aren't a celebrity or an industry leader who has millions of followers or is a household name, that means Leadership is one of the worst categories for your book. Instead, (the data shows) you would be exponentially better off writing an Idea-Centric book. And the categories where Idea-Centric books excel are Insights/Thinking and Personal Development (where your personal standing is second priority to the quality of your ideas).

Scenario B: Celebrity Leader

Now let's say you're Steve Kerr, former NBA champion and legendary head coach of the Golden State Warriors.

You're Steve Kerr and you want to write a book. A traditional publisher is likely going to recommend writing a Leadership book—and according to our analysis, in this scenario, this is a good idea. The Leadership category benefits from Author-Centric ideas ("I'm the head coach of NBA champions, here's how we do it...") and Author-Centric covers ("Look at me, I'm Steve Kerr!"). Lots of people want to learn about Leadership from Steve Kerr. Not very many people want to learn about Leadership from No-Name CEO whose public standing doesn't make their leadership skills immediately recognizable and apparent.

Now, here's the nuance:

Traditional publishers love publishing books from celebrities and well-known industry thought leaders (especially ones with large digital audiences) because they know it's easier to sell books from someone the world already knows vs doesn't know. But what doesn't get talked about (or isn't conscious) is how and when this model fails. Not every celebrity book is a home run.

For example, Billie Eilish has over 100 million Instagram followers, and published a book in 2019 that ended up selling less than 100,000 copies in its first year on bookshelves. How does that happen? The answer goes back to one of our Pirate Mantras: categories make brands, not the other way around. And when you are a celebrity or well-known thought leader, it is very easy to think the reason people buy your book is because of who "you" are—when in reality, what makes readers want to buy your book is based on whether or not your standing enhances the quality of the category *and speaks directly to the reader.* (Categories are about customers, their problems and their opportunities. Brands are about you. And no one cares about you. They only care about themselves. And the book sales data proves it.)

Steve Kerr's book on Leadership makes sense.

Steve Kerr's book on the future of the music industry doesn't.

Why?

Because his standing only matters in the context of the right topic category. And simply saying, "I'm famous" or "Lots of people know who I am" isn't enough to make people care (or move copies). This also underscores that being famous does not make you successful. Being famous *for* something that makes a difference to *others* is what makes you successful. (If you really want to screw yourself up, become famous and poor. We know people like this. They have large social followings, have been promoted and exposed heavily on TV, but they are not known for a niche they own. They have made little impact for others, so it is almost impossible to monetize their fame. Getting asked for your autograph while out to a dinner you cannot afford will scramble your cerebellum.)

The missed opportunity is when publishers or someone with significant authority settles for writing a book that is "all about them" instead of ascending further up the 7 Best-Selling Book Categories. A book about Leadership from Steve Kerr is fine. But (in this hypothetical example) an Insights/Thinking book about how Steve Kerr used data, a new mental model, and motivation to change the game of basketball is even more interesting, more timeless, and has more pricing power. And ascending further: a book about how Steve Kerr used orthogonal thinking to discover a goldmine of opportunity—AND HOW YOU CAN TOO—would put the book in Personal Development territory and have the highest likelihood of scaling, remaining relevant for the longest period of time, and have the most pricing power.

Regardless of what topic you want to write about, you should always consider how you can execute that topic through an Insights/Thinking or Personal Development lens—if you want your ideas to scale, and if you want to make the most money as a writer.

If you don't care about your ideas scaling, and if you don't care about maximizing your earnings (meaning both impact and financial upside are not motivators for you), then write whatever kind of book you want and call yourself an "author."

Just don't be surprised when copies of your book rust on the shelf.

The First 3 Steps Of Writing A Best-Selling Business Book

Let's recap what we've discussed so far:

Step 1: Choose Your Starting Category

Before you even begin writing your book (or "scaling" an idea of any kind), you first need to decide which of the 7 best-selling, most-scalable categories you are going to play in—and why:

- Personal Development
- Personal Finance
- Insights/Thinking
- Leadership
- Case Study/Allegory
- Functional Excellence
- Relationships

Step 2: Idea-Centric or Author-Centric

Next, be honest with yourself:

Question: Are you a celebrity? Are you at the absolute height of your industry and would everyone inside that industry be able to recognize you on the street? (Michelle Obama's book, *Becoming*, is a memoir that has sold over 14 million copies. And by the time it came out, she was one of the highest profile people in the world—and as a couple, the Obamas were the "most admired couple in the world." Are you at that level?) Or are you a no-name writer, entrepreneur, or industry thought leader? Be radically honest with yourself. If you are, it might be OK to write an Author-Centric book that leans on your personal experience and social standing. But if not, then you're better off writing an Idea-Centric book instead.

Question: Would you care if someone else "stole" your idea? Or built upon your idea and added their own twist? Or took your idea and ran with it in a different direction? This gets at the heart of whether you are a missionary or a mercenary. Everyone cares a little bit, but if you *really* care (like you would be furious to see someone else building on your work), then you lean more Author-Centric. You need to be the star of the show. However, if you are ultimately glad people were helped, and you see other people building on your work as a net-positive for the world, then you are likely more Idea-Centric. You just care that the information helps people. Whether you get "all the credit" isn't as important as the mission you are on.

If the book you want to write is Idea-Centric, the categories best suited to "scale" your idea are:

- Personal Development
- Insights/Thinking
- Case Study/Allegory
- Relationships

If the book you want to write is Author-Centric, the categories best suited to "scale" your idea are:

- Personal Finance
- Leadership
- Functional Excellence

It's worth remembering that Idea-Centric books are typically more scalable than Author-Centric books because when you write an Author-Centric book, your pool of prospective readers is limited to the number of people who know who you are. Whereas anyone can write an interesting Idea-Centric book, and if the idea is compelling, new, and different, that idea can take on a life of its own—and oftentimes outgrow the author. For example, nobody knew who James Clear was when he wrote *Atomic Habits*. That is an Idea-Centric book that did not require the author's credibility in order to resonate with readers.

So, even if you want to write an Author-Centric book, consider how you might be able to give the spotlight to the idea itself.

Step 3: Ascend To a Superior Category

Finally, how "scalable" do you want your book to be?

To increase your total addressable market of readers, think about how you can ascend up these 7 best-selling categories to maximize your impact and financial upside:

- If you are writing a Personal Finance book, can you make the category bigger and write it as an Insights/Thinking book geared toward a financial audience? Or, even better, can you make it a Personal Development book about how money habits can unlock more universal, desirable life outcomes (happiness, freedom, status, mental calm, emotional acceptance, etc.)?

- If you are writing a Relationships book, can you make the category bigger and conduct your own survey or clinical study so the book presents new and different Insights/Thinking? Or, even better, can you give unique, actionable Personal Development takeaways for the reader?

- If you are writing a Leadership book, can you make it a "science of leadership" book so it becomes about new Insights/Thinking? Or, even better, can you combine your new leadership science with different, actionable takeaways for the reader—so by the time they finish reading, they will have the necessary skills to be a legendary leader, too?

- If you are writing a book full of Case Study/Allegories, can you minimize the timely aspects of these case studies and instead focus on the wisdom (Insights/Thinking) that will stand the test of time? Even better, can you help the reader implement this timeless wisdom in their own lives (Personal Development)?

- If you are writing a Functional Excellence book, can you minimize the timely How To advice and examples that will only be relevant for a few years (if that), and instead focus on the underlying principles of success that will remain relevant for a much longer time horizon?

Again: all roads lead back to Insights/Thinking and Personal Development. In order to increase your chances of writing a best-seller and presenting an idea that "scales" to millions of readers, you must either present new and different ways of seeing the world, or give the reader clear and actionable (Obvious/Non-Obvious) steps they can take to succeed in the world.

The magic combination is to do both at the same time.

The "Y Do You Write" Framework

Notice how all of these "thinking" decisions need to be made before you write a single word of your book!

(Thinking about thinking is the most important kind of thinking.)

Once you have worked through these first 3 steps, you will find yourself at a fork in the road:

- **To The Left:** Obvious creation
- **To The Right:** Non-Obvious creation

We call this the "Y Do You Write" framework because in order for readers to understand what kind of idea you are trying to get them to "buy into," you need to have perfect clarity around whether you are writing an Obvious or Non-Obvious book. This is what dictates whether readers buy your book and devour it, buy your book but don't read it, or don't buy your book at all.

There are 4 combinations of Obvious and Non-Obvious ideas:

Obvious Problem, Obvious Solution

Obvious problems are already commonly understood, and Obvious solutions to Obvious problems are commodities.

For example: an Obvious problem would be "I don't want to clean my house." And an Obvious solution would be to hire a cleaner. Since this is an Obvious problem, you don't have to work very hard to educate people who have this problem (they already know they do). And because so many Obvious solutions exist, most cleaning jobs pay minimum wage or slightly above.

In the business "thinking" world, an Obvious problem would be, "I don't know the first thing about marketing," and an Obvious solution would be "marketing made simple" or "how to get started in marketing." This sort of Obvious content lends itself well to beginners, but that's where the buck stops. How many times do you need to read (and re-read) "a simple system" or "a step-by-step guide" for the same Obvious problem? (Scroll through the Marketing section on Amazon and you'll find tens of thousands of books that essentially all say the same three things: know your customer, build your brand, measure results. *Blah, blah, blah.*) Since this sort of content is typically one-and-done and easily substitutable—anyone with moderate competence in a given subject matter can write "a step-by-step guide"—it quickly becomes indefensible.

So as you begin writing your book (or article, or Twitter Thread, or LinkedIn post), be aware of whether you are tackling an Obvious problem with an Obvious solution. If you are, a siren should go off in your brain: **you are creating a commodity.**

And even if your work attracts attention, it will be short lived.

Which means, in order to increase the shelf life of your work, you should make an effort to find or create a Non-Obvious solution to this Obvious problem.

Obvious Problem, Non-Obvious Solution

Non-Obvious solutions to Obvious problems are joyfully surprising.

For example: an Obvious problem for many people is that when they climb into bed at night, they feel hot. And when you feel hot, it's hard to fall asleep. We all know this problem, and when we feel it, we think of Obvious solutions:

- Turn on the AC
- Position a fan by the bed
- Set a timer on your AC so the room is cold long before you climb into bed
- Etc.

But because these are Obvious solutions to an Obvious problem, we don't value them very highly because none of them are surprising. Imagine you hired an air conditioning technician to come to your house and he said, "You're hot at night? My solution would be to turn on the AC. That'll be $40, please." You'd practically shout back, "Are you kidding me? I could have thought of that!" As we said above, Obvious solutions to Obvious problems are commodities so we don't value them very highly—logically or financially.

Non-Obvious solutions to Obvious problems, however, are unique. They make us tilt our heads and ask genuinely, "Woah, how come I didn't think of that?" For example, a Non-Obvious solution to the Obvious I'm-too-hot-at-night problem is to buy an 8 Sleep Mattress—which is a smart mattress with temperature control. It connects to your smartphone and you can select how cold you want your bed to be when you fall asleep (and how cold you want it to stay all through the night).

An AC technician costs $40 per hour.

An 8 Sleep mattress costs $4,000.

Which means, financially speaking, we value Non-Obvious solutions to Obvious problems upwards of 100x more.

So, if you want to write a legendary business book, you want to consider how you can present Non-Obvious solutions to Obvious problems. This is the vast majority of the books on our Top 444 list.

- "A **completely new way** of approaching your morning routine..."

- "**Groundbreaking science** that will change the way you
  nurture relationships in your life..."
- "An **unconventional approach** to living a happy life..."
- "The **unspoken** art of timeless leadership..."

All of these small descriptor words subtly tell the reader, "Check
this out. This is a Non-Obvious solution to an Obvious problem." And
because Non-Obvious solutions are surprising, we can't help but gravitate
towards them.

We want to open the surprise!

(Of course, the content of the book has to actually be Non-Obvious.
If your title or subtle hints at Non-Obvious insights or action steps, but
then the content is 100% Obvious, the reader is going to be severely disappointed.)

As we wrote about in The Content Pyramid, if you want your idea
to scale quickly and you want it to scale as soon as possible, you want to
play at the intersection of providing Non-Obvious solutions to Obvious
problems. Because people already know they have a problem (you don't
have to educate them on it), and people have likely tried all the Obvious
solutions already—which means they are a "starving crowd" desperate
for a fix. So if you can present a Non-Obvious, easy-to-grasp solution,
they are going to gravitate to it quickly.

Which presents a double-edged sword.

The benefit of Non-Obvious solutions to Obvious problems is that
the world is more open to them, sooner.

But the problem with Non-Obvious solutions to Obvious problems
is they are hard to make defensible for a long period of time.

How many new books are written each year with a "new, groundbreaking, unconventional" approach to productivity? Or relationships?
Or wealth? Once the world catches wind of your Non-Obvious solution
to an Obvious, painful, urgent problem, the jig is up—and what was once
Non-Obvious very quickly becomes conventional wisdom and Obvious.

One of the clearest examples of this in the publishing industry is when Jen Sincero published *You Are A Badass* (2013) and Mark Manson published *The Subtle Art of Not Giving a F*ck* (2016). The Obvious problem up until this point was that the self-help industry was mostly geared toward serious readers—people who wanted to read about psychology or spirituality. Until these two writers came along and presented a Non-Obvious solution: let's not make self-help all serious. Let's just talk about how to not give a fuck!

And what happened?

These books became two of the best-selling books of the past decade.

Of course, it didn't take very long for a zillion other writers to pile in—thinking that as long as they put an expletive in their book title ("Hey! I can provide that Non-Obvious solution too!"), they were going to sell millions of copies. But the law of Category Design tells us this is false. There can only be one "Fuck" Category King. And 99% of these writers wrote mediocre, undifferentiated books in an effort to catch the "Fuck" demand created by Mark Manson—and as a result barely moved any "Fucking" copies.

So while a Non-Obvious solution to an Obvious problem can be effective in grabbing people's attention in the short term, don't be surprised when other people follow in your footsteps—and your Non-Obvious solution quickly becomes Obvious.

Non-Obvious Problem, Obvious Solution

If you want fame and fortune now, give people Non-Obvious solutions to Obvious problems.

(Everyone loves a quick, simple, surprising answer.)

However, if you want to become known for a niche you own, and you want your reign to last decades (or even lifetimes), then you want to be in the business of educating the world on Non-Obvious problems— **problems they didn't know they had until you came along and opened**

their eyes. And then you want to give them an Obvious, candy-coated solution they can use right away to solve this newfound problem they now can't get out of their mind.

For example: Category Design (or a lack thereof) is a Non-Obvious problem.

Most companies and creators know when they need help with email marketing, or need help running paid ads, or need help improving their landing page copy. These are all Obvious problems. What most companies and creators do not know, however, is whether or not they dominate a category. It doesn't even cross their mind—until a Category Designer comes along and asks the question: "What is your Category Design? What niche are you dominating? Are you catching existing demand or creating new demand? What decisions are you making that will allow you to consciously design & dominate your chosen category for the next 10 or 20 years?"

The result here should be Obvious (no pun intended): educating people on Non-Obvious problems they didn't know they had is *harder* than mirroring an existing, Obvious problem. Non-Obvious problems require education and explanation. They require context and examples. As a result, it takes a bit longer to get people onboard.

However...

Once you educate someone about a Non-Obvious problem and the lightbulb goes off in their head, they can't unsee it. They are changed forever. Everywhere they go, they see this problem popping up over and over again. (We get this feedback from people who read Category Pirates—"Categories are everywhere!") As their awareness of this Non-Obvious problem increases, so too does their desire for an Obvious solution: education, information, consultation, a product or service, etc. And since you were the one who educated them about the problem, they assume you are the best person (or the only person) to help them solve it!

He or she who frames the problem owns the solution.

Even though it's harder (and takes longer) to educate the world on a problem they didn't know they had, the timeline of your category dominance will last tremendously longer. Nassim Nicholas Taleb's book, *The Black Swan*, is a prime example. This book educated the world on a Non-Obvious problem called "the characteristics of a highly improbable event." This book has sold a fraction of the copies of other more Obvious books, however *The Black Swan* will continue to be read and referenced over a much longer time horizon. In fact, it will be very hard for any writer to say, "I'm going to write about highly improbable events too" without immediately being compared to Nassim Nicholas Taleb and *The Black Swan*.

So again: if you want fame and fortune now, provide Non-Obvious solutions to Obvious problems—but realize your shelf life will be shorter.

But if you are willing to postpone fame & fortune a bit, and would rather build a more defensible moat around your niche (and optimize for impact, contribution, and legacy), then educate the world on Non-Obvious problems and give them simple, actionable, Obvious solutions they can put into practice right away to solve the problem they now know they have (because of you).

Non-Obvious Problem, Non-Obvious Solution

If Obvious solutions to Obvious problems are commodities, then Non-Obvious solutions to Non-Obvious problems are so smart they're stupid.

This is what happens when a mathematician solves some massively valuable equation but dies alone and forgotten. Or when a historian comes to an earth-shattering realization but never gets celebrated beyond their inner circle of academics. Smart as they may be, they struggle to make their idea "scale." And the reason is because—by accident, by choice, or by ego—they make it difficult for other people to step foot into their world. They communicate in overly smart, convoluted ways to the point where everyday people have no idea what they are talking about. They want the world to think they are geniuses. (But proving something about you and educating people are very different things.) In this type of content, there's no "Obvious" entrypoint. And as a result, very few people pay attention. They don't know why it's a problem (Non-Obvious), and even if they did, they can't wrap their mind around the solution (also Non-Obvious).

But legendary Non-Obvious thinkers find a way to communicate in such a way that they meet people where they are and take them *FROM* what they know *TO* a new and different way.

We notice a lot of academics use the Non-Obvious problem/ Non-Obvious solution intersection as a way of distancing themselves from "the average person" and validating their own ego. They almost take pride in the fact that "not everyone gets it." And yes, some complicated topics require the questioning of Non-Obvious problems and the consideration of Non-Obvious solutions, simultaneously. We just want to point out that if you stay here, you will fail to give your audience an Obvious entrypoint into your work—and your idea is never going to scale.

Non-Obvious/Non-Obvious is a recipe for disaster.

Nobody is going to "get it."

So, Y Do You Write?

The takeaway here should be... Obvious.

If you want your book to resonate with a large number of people, your idea to "scale," AND for your idea to be defensible and have a meaningful shelf life, then you need to either:

- Provide people with Obvious solutions to Non-Obvious problems
- Or educate people on Non-Obvious problems they didn't

know they had, and then give them easy-to-use, immediately actionable Obvious solutions (it's no fun reading a book that makes you aware of a problem in your life but doesn't tell you how to solve it!)
And this decision should inform both the title and subtitle of your book.

The Cover Says It All

Can you judge a book by its cover?

According to our analysis, you can.

Through this new lens, you can tell a lot about the content of a book long before you even open up to chapter one. Category potential, Idea-Centric vs Author-Centric, shelf life, Obvious vs Non-Obvious, all of these qualities are fairly easy to recognize through this new lens. As a result, even just by reading the title and subtitle of a best-selling book, you can quickly discern whether or not it's worth your time—and if it is, how come and why.

For example, let's walk through a handful of best-selling titles from our analysis (chosen at random) and see what we can glean just from the title and subtitle and a glance at the book's description:

Total Money Makeover: A Proven Plan For Financial Fitness

By Dave Ramsey

- Personal Finance book
- Ascends up the 7 major categories by steering it into Personal Development ("A Proven Plan")
- Author-Centric, Not Idea-Centric (This book isn't about a groundbreaking new way of thinking about money. It's

about what Dave Ramsey thinks you should do with your
money! It's "proven" because Dave Ramsey says so.)

- Obvious problem = "I have money problems."
- Obvious solution = "Give me a proven plan, step-by-step."

Dave Ramsey's books have sold several million copies combined, but
Total Money Makeover is his highest-selling book by a wide margin.
However, it doesn't take a rocket surgeon to see that even after selling
millions of copies, his work is easily substitutable—which means his
Obvious solutions to Obvious problems will become more and more
commoditized as time goes on. "How do you pay off your debt? You
have to be disciplined, save a little bit extra each month, and pay it off."
Obvious/Obvious.

Now let's compare this book with another Personal Finance book:

Rich Dad Poor Dad: What The Rich Teach Their Kids About Money That The Poor And Middle Class Do Not!
By Robert T. Kiyosaki

- Personal Finance book
- Ascends up the 7 major categories by making it a Personal
  Development book
- Bonus points for incorporating a timeless Allegory/Fable
  here that makes it feel like these stories/insights will "live
  forever."
- Idea-Centric, not Author-Centric (Nothing about this
  book title implies Robert T. Kiyosaki is the main character, despite the entire book being about his personal story.
  This is the perfect example of letting the "idea" have the
  spotlight in an effort to get your story, lessons, and idea to
  "scale" beyond yourself.)
- Obvious problem = "Why are some people rich and some
  people poor?"

- Non-Obvious solution = "Because the rich know things
  about money, and teach these secret rules to their kids,
  that the poor and middle class don't know about!"

Rich Dad Poor Dad is maybe one of the greatest book titles of all time—but not for the reasons most people think. It's not the fact that it's a "clever title" that makes it so effective. It's that *Rich Dad Poor Dad* implies two different paths and two very different transformations (similar to one of the greatest sales letters of all time for *The Wall Street Journal*, "A Tale Of Two Young Men"), forcing the reader to ask themselves, "Which one am I?". In addition, *Rich Dad Poor Dad* doesn't lean on Kiyosaki's experience level at all—it's one hundred percent Idea-Centric—and provides a "surprising" Non-Obvious answer to one of the most universal Obvious questions of all time: "How come I'm not rich?" To which Kiyosaki provides a Non-Obvious and seductive answer: "It's your dad's fault!" While this is primarily a Personal Finance book, he dips into the Relationship category by offering you a chance to "choose a new dad" when it comes to money.

Each of these subtle decisions, reflected in the title and subtitle, are what dictate the scalability and resonance of the book.

Unfortunately, Kiyosaki's publisher didn't have this framework when titling all the rest of his books. Every single book published after *Rich Dad Poor Dad* starts with *Rich Dad* in the title. Without even realizing it, Kiyosaki and his publisher went from being Idea-Centric to Author-Centric, changing the sell to readers from, "You'll love this idea!" to "You'll love Robert!" (We humans are so self-centered that when Nicolaus Copernicus told us the earth revolves around the sun—not the other way around—his work was banned!) In Category Design this is called "line extension," where you take your brand and try to extend its credibility into neighboring niches—and it's a cardinal sin. It should come as no surprise that all of these derivatives of *Rich Dad Poor Dad* drastically undersold the original.

Remember: categories make brands, not the other way around.
Let's walk through a few more examples:

Never Split The Difference: Negotiating As If Your Life Depended On It
By Chris Voss

- Personal Development book ("How To Negotiate")
- Idea-Centric, Not Author-Centric (Nothing about the title leans on the fact that its author is speaking from experience as a former FBI hostage negotiator, allowing the "idea" itself to have the spotlight.)
- Obvious problem = "How can I get better at negotiating?"
- Non-Obvious solution = "Negotiate like your life depends on it."

Of all the negotiation advice you've heard in your life, "negotiate like your life depends on it" is different and surprising. This is the beauty of providing Non-Obvious answers and solutions to Obvious, everyday problems.

And while it's interesting to know the author of the book is a former FBI hostage negotiator, the reason people buy this book (and the reason it has sold so many copies) is because the book isn't about Chris Voss. The book is about the reader, and what they can learn about negotiation.

Idea-Centric vs Author-Centric.

Fooled By Randomness: The Hidden Role Of Chance In Life And In The Markets
By Nicholas Nassim Taleb

- Insights/Thinking book
- Idea-Centric, Not Author-Centric (Taleb's reputation

isn't mentioned or implied anywhere in the title.)

- Obvious problem = "Why do random things happen?"
- Non-Obvious solution = "Things aren't always as they
  seem—and there's a hidden reason why!"

Notice how if you are someone who has thought about this subject before (you are aware of this Obvious problem in your life), then Taleb's teasing of a Non-Obvious solution feels intriguing to you. "Ah! I haven't thought of this before!"

That tingly feeling is what you give readers when you provide Non-Obvious solutions to Obvious problems.

Crossing The Chasm: Marketing And Selling Disruptive Products To Mainstream Customers
By Geoffrey A. Moore

- Insights/Thinking book (Doesn't tell you "how to DO"
  as much as "how to THINK" about the subject)
- Idea-Centric, Not Author-Centric (Nothing about this
  title has anything to do with the author's background.)
- Non-Obvious problem = "I know how to sell Obvious
  products to mainstream customers, but how do I sell
  Non-Obvious products to people who don't know they
  need them yet?"
- Obvious solution = "Read this book!" (From the description: "The bible for bringing cutting-edge products to
  larger markets.")

Crossing The Chasm is a great example of a book that has to do some education on the problem before it provides a solution. The problem here is that most entrepreneurs and executives assume if they make a great product then everyone will just "get it." But when you are creating a product the world isn't ready for yet (Non-Obvious), this isn't true.

Once you (the reader) see, understand, and believe you have this problem ("Hey! I have a disruptive product the world might not be ready for yet too!") you can't get the problem out of your head—which causes you to start to search for a solution and buy the book. "Not sure how to market and sell disruptive products to mainstream customers? Inside, I explain to you how to think about marketing and selling disruptive products to mainstream customers."

Non-Obvious problem, Obvious solution.

Blink: The Power Of Thinking Without Thinking
By Malcolm Gladwell

- Insights/Thinking book
- Idea-Centric, Not Author-Centric (*Blink* was published after Gladwell already became a bestseller from his first book, *The Tipping Point*. Props to him for not making the mistake of pivoting from Idea-Centric to Author-Centric!)
- Non-Obvious problem = "Did you know you are making big decisions on instinct without realizing it?"
- Obvious solution = "Learn how to trust your gut!"

Malcolm Gladwell is an archetypal Non-Obvious writer. Nobody wakes up in the morning and asks themselves, "I wonder what I'm thinking when I'm making snap decisions? Am I thinking at all?" These are Non-Obvious questions Gladwell loves tackling in his books—and the reason they're so fun to read is because he answers them in Obvious ways, told through stories.

From the book's description: "In *Blink* we meet the psychologist who has learned to predict whether a marriage will last, based on a few minutes of observing a couple; the tennis coach who knows when a player will double-fault before the racket even makes contact with the ball; the antiquities experts who recognize a fake at a glance."

When you finish reading one of Gladwell's books, you don't really walk away with anything actionable you can apply to your own life. (He doesn't ascend up the 7 categories and step into Personal Development.) However, these simple explanations to complicated questions are what make his books memorable—and also why he constantly faces criticism from the Non-Obvious/Non-Obvious scientific community.

"If my books appear oversimplified, then you shouldn't read them," Gladwell said in an interview with The Guardian (2013).

What's Worth Reading and Buying

The reason we want you to have this lens is because you can tell a lot about a book just by looking closely at its title, subtitle, and giving the description a quick skim. Pirate Christopher and his podcast team receive countless pitches a week from PR people trying to get their clients on his show, "Follow Your Different." This lens makes it exponentially easier to figure out who to say "Yes" to and who to politely decline. Because the truth is, most business books and most "thought leaders" live in the Obvious/Obvious world—no matter how many accolades and awards they list out in their pitch emails. They are easy "No Thank Yous" for a podcast focused on finding Non-Obvious guests. (Recently after learning this framework, a CMO we know said, "Shit! Everything we produce is Obvious/Obvious!" Which is why you almost never hear someone say that a piece of corporate content is legendary.)

In addition, many of us have what is called "book guilt." We know reading is important. We have bookshelves filled with books we want to read, or feel like we should. But might it be that we buy books we think will help us, only to read the first page and be let down?

Here's how to minimize book guilt by prioritizing the books you've already bought and making smarter choices about what to buy and when going forward.

If you are a beginner looking for a place to start (in a given subject matter), a book that speaks to your Obvious problem ("I don't know where to start") and promises Obvious solutions ("a step-by-step guide") is for you. However, if you are not a beginner and find yourself still buying Obvious/Obvious books, stop. There's nothing "new" in there for you (no matter how respected the author seems). You're wasting your money.

If you are beyond a beginner (in a given subject matter), or are just looking for something new and interesting, a book that still speaks to your familiar Obvious problem ("I'd love to learn more about X") but instead gives you a surprising solution ("a little-known strategy") is right up your alley. You can tell someone is a Superconsumer of a given topic when their bookshelf is lined with Non-Obvious solutions to an Obvious problem. (Pirate Cole has an entire collection of books on writing and copywriting, each providing different Non-Obvious solutions to the age-old Obvious problem, "How do I become a great writer?") These also make for fun gifts to friends, family members, and co-workers who are also interested in this same topic—because you are giving them a "surprising" and new solution to a problem they think they know so well.

If you are an expert in a given domain, then Obvious/Obvious and most Obvious/Non-Obvious books aren't going to do it for you. Even the "surprising" Non-Obvious solutions won't give you any dopamine. "I know all of this," you'll say. Instead, what you're really looking for is someone smart to educate you on a Non-Obvious problem you didn't know you had.

And only if you are a Superconsumer, and an expert of a given domain, are you going to consider anything remotely Non-Obvious/Non-Obvious. But even still, you are most likely going to end up chucking the book across the room for not making it Obvious in some way.

When we buy and read books that align with what we're looking for, we're elated.

And when we buy and try to read books that don't, we're upset.

This lens should help you find what you're looking for—before you even read the first page.

The Best-Selling Title & Subtitle Formula: 5 Laws Of Scalability

Which leads us to the big question:

"What should the title of my book be?"

Every single writer (and publisher) obsesses over the book title. And rightfully so. As we hope you gleaned from the above, your book's title can make or break the "scalability" of your idea. The content inside could be amazing, but if your title doesn't speak clearly to the reader, they're never going to feel inspired to pick up a copy.

So, we want to give you a framework for making sure your book title accomplishes its goal: to attract the right readers and repel the wrong ones.

(Remember: legendary brands force a choice, not a comparison.)

Here are the 5 laws of scalability:

Law #1: Clear, Not Clever

There is an epidemic among writers, and it's to be "clever."

Ask any first-time author what they think the title of their book should be, and 99% of them will say back a clever title. This is because we grow up thinking "clever" and "creative" are synonyms—and they're not. The writer believes that when the reader (aka their mom or dad) sees their clever book title, they are going to STOP, and they are going to say to themselves, "Holy shit. This writer is so clever. I am amazed. I have to stop everything I'm doing and start reading this book right now." (We're being facetious, of course.)

In reality, the opposite happens: a reader comes across your "clever" title, doesn't immediately "get it", and two seconds later their attention is on something else.

So, don't try to be clever.

Just be clear.

- Does this book solve an Obvious problem with an Obvious solution?
- Does this book solve an Obvious problem with a Non-Obvious solution?
- Does this book point out a Non-Obvious problem and solve it with an Obvious solution?
- Does this book point out a Non-Obvious problem and solve it with a Non-Obvious solution?

Law #2: Use Language That Signals The Primary "Benefit"

Different combinations of Obvious/Non-Obvious require different language.

The benefit of reading a book that provides an Obvious solution to an Obvious problem is that it's simple. Easy to understand. Broken down into steps. Etc.

So, use this language in the title or subtitle!

- "A Simple System"
- "Easy Exercises"
- "A Step-By-Step Approach"

The benefit of reading a book that provides a Non-Obvious solution to an Obvious problem is that it's surprising. Unconventional. Unknown, until now.

So, use this language in the title or subtitle!

- "The Surprising Truth"
- "An Unconventional Approach"

- "The Little-Known Strategy"

The benefit of reading a book that educates you about a Non-Obvious problem you didn't know you were experiencing, and then gives you an Obvious answer or solution to solve it, is that it's eye-opening. Shocking. Mind-boggling.

So, use this language in the title or subtitle!

- "An Eye-Opening Perspective"
- "This Shocking Study"
- "A Mind-Boggling Research Report"

And the benefit of reading a book that educates you about a Non-Obvious problem you didn't know you were experiencing, and then gives you a Non-Obvious answer or solution to solve it is, well, there is none. *Try not to write a Non-Obvious/Non-Obvious book.*

When the language you use corresponds to the "benefit" the reader experiences consuming that type of book, a siren goes off in their subconscious mind that tells them: "Hey! This is for you! This is what you've been looking for!"

So don't overcomplicate it.

Say what the reader is already thinking back to them.

Law #3: Title & Subtitle Should Mirror Obvious & Non-Obvious Pairing

Similarly, the Obvious/Non-Obvious combination you choose should be reflected in the main title & subtitle.

If you are writing an Obvious/Obvious book, then your Main Title & Subtitle should be Obvious/Obvious.

For example:

- 17 Essential Qualities of a Team Player: Becoming the Kind of Person Every Team Wants
- The 9 Steps to Financial Freedom: Practical and Spiritual Steps So You Can Stop Worrying

- The Power of a Positive Team: Proven Principles and Practices That Make Great Teams Great

If you are writing an Obvious/Non-Obvious book, then your Main Title & Subtitle should be some combination of Obvious/Non-Obvious.

For example:

- Made To Stick: Why Some Ideas Survive And Others Die
- Drive: The Surprising Truth About What Motivates Us
- The Millionaire Next Door: The Surprising Secrets Of America's Wealthy

If you are writing a Non-Obvious/Obvious book, then your Main Title & Subtitle should be some combination of Non-Obvious/Obvious.

For example:

- *Freakonomics: A Rogue Economist Explores The Hidden Side Of Everything*
- *The Smartest Guys In the Room: The Amazing Rise And Scandalous Fall of Enron*

And if you are writing a Non-Obvious/Non-Obvious book, then you should make either the Main Title or Subtitle Obvious (in some way) to give readers an entrypoint into your work.

(What is this actually about?)

Law #4: Languaging In The Main Title

By a wide margin, the vast majority of best-selling books use Non-Obvious, more "sticky" (sometimes veering into the territory of "clever") main titles, followed by extremely Obvious, straightforward "How To" subtitles. While we certainly saw examples where this was inverted, such as Jordan B. Peterson's book, *12 Rules For Life: An Antidote To Chaos*, these are outliers. You can do either, however the important takeaway is to avoid (at all costs) a Non-Obvious ("What does this mean?") main title followed by a Non-Obvious ("What does this mean?") subtitle. (A mistake we used to make a lot!)

You have no idea what the book *Start With Why* is about until you read its subtitle: *How Great Leaders Inspire Everyone To Take Action*. If *Start With Why*'s subtitle had been something also Non-Obvious, such as *Start With Why: Leadership Through Darkness*, the book would have sold a fraction of the copies—because neither the Main Title or the Subtitle is Obvious and tells the reader: "This is what this book is about."

Coming up with an effective main title is a whole art in itself.

Since so many best-selling books have short, quippy Main Titles, aspiring authors and industry thought leaders try to do the same.

For example:

- Start With Why
- Built To Last
- Made To Stick
- Good To Great
- Zero To One
- Tribe Of Mentors
- The Fifth Discipline
- Crossing The Chasm
- The Innovator's Dilemma

And so on.

(Can you "hear" the cadence all these Main Titles share in common?)

The mistake many writers, thought leaders, and publishers make, however, is mirroring *the sound of the cadence* and not the Languaging— the strategic use of language to make the reader "think" something very specific. **An effective title isn't three words with a bouncy rhythm.** An effective title is one that makes the Obvious/Non-Obvious combination of the book clear, unique, and memorable to the reader.

Here are a few formulas we spotted from our analysis that you can use as templates when coming up with a title for your own book.

Formula: Main Title Is A Synonym For The Book's Big Idea

One way to "hook" the reader's attention using Languaging is to make the Main Title of your book a simple word or phrase that is a synonym for the book's big idea.

For example:

*Drive: The Surprising Truth About What **Motivates** Us*

The big idea in this book is that what motivates us as human beings isn't what we think. OK, what's a synonym for "motivation?" Because the book title *Motivation: The Surprising Truth About What Motivates Us* just doesn't seem very compelling, now does it? Ah! "Drive" is a synonym for "motivation!"

Wabam—now you look like a brilliant author.

Here's another example:

*Multipliers: How The Best Leaders **Make Everyone Smarter***

The big idea in this book is that the best leaders make everyone around them smarter. (Notice how the subtitle is literally the elevator pitch? That's the signal of an amazing, Obvious subtitle.) But a book title like *Smarter: How The Best Leaders Make Everyone Smarter* just doesn't have a very nice ring to it. So, what's a synonym for "make everyone smarter?" Well, when you make everyone around you smarter, you effectively become a force multiplier.

Ah! Brilliant!

When coming up with a title for your own book, use this simple framework: take the book's big idea and reduce it down to a single word or phrase. Then choose a synonym—something that means the same thing, but is a little different. (The magic line you are trying to walk here is using new Languaging that instantly sounds familiar.)

Formula: Main Title Is A Transformation/Outcome

- The 4-Hour Work Week
- Rich Dad Poor Dad
- Hooked

Whenever your main title can represent the transformation the reader is going to experience after reading, you're in the money. When you hear *The 4-Hour Work Week,* you think, "Hey! I want a 4-hour work week!" That's a transformation. Or when you hear *Rich Dad Poor Dad,* you think, "Hey! I had a Poor Dad. Give me a Rich Dad!" That's a transformation. Or when you hear *Hooked,* you think, "Hey! I want to build software products people get hooked on!" That's a transformation—subtly signaling where the reader is today, and where they're going to end up after they read this book.

These types of titles are few and far between—because truthfully, most people who write books are more Author-Centric (ego) than they realize, and so they aren't really in the business of helping the reader facilitate a transformation. They're more interested in proving how smart they are and being seen as the expert. As a result, the title is less about the transformation the reader is going to experience, and more about the transformation the author is going to experience ("Look at me! Now I'm an author!").

Formula: Main Title Is The Golden Rule Inside The Book

Another formula is using the golden rule from the book as the main title to hook the reader's attention.

- Never Split The Difference
- Leaders Eat Last
- You Don't Need A Title To Be A Leader
- Never Eat Alone

Each of these main titles is essentially the big takeaway. The pro of using this formula is that the reader immediately gets a sense of what your book is about. The con, of course, is that it sort of gives away the morale of the story. Do you really need to read 250 pages on why networking over meals is a good idea—and why you should "never eat alone?" Not really. You basically get the point of the book just by reading the title. (Most business books are one idea stretched across 300 pages like an old, out of shape Stretch Armstrong.)

We recommend using this formula as a forcing function for the content of the book. Use "the golden rule" you are passing along to readers in your book as the title itself, but then make sure that the content inside over-delivers. If the content of your book is basically just lots of examples and reasons why the reader should "never eat alone," your book has the value of a paperweight.

Formula: Word Image

- *Purple Cow*: *Transform Your Business By Being Remarkable*
- *The Black Swan*: *The Impact Of The Highly Improbable*
- *Soup*: *A Recipe To Create A Culture Of Greatness*

Another formula is to take the big idea from your book and then pick a word image that represents that idea and make that your main title.

For example, *Purple Cow* by Seth Godin is about how businesses can create something "phenomenal, counterintuitive, exciting, and flat-out unbelievable" such that they go from being a normal cow (invisible in a crowd) to being a Purple Cow: noticeable even from 1,000 miles away.

Word Images require a bit more explanation in order to "get it," however if your word image is successful at encapsulating your big idea, they become very sticky. Nearly everyone in marketing has heard of the term Purple Cow, regardless of whether or not they've read the book. That's a pretty powerful word-of-mouth mechanism.

Formula: Invent A Word (Name & Claim Your Idea/ Category)

Finally, you can invent a new word altogether.

For example:

Freakonomics: *A Rogue Economist Explores The Hidden Side Of Everything*

"Freak" is a word, and "economics" is a word, but *Freakonomics* was a new word authors Steven D. Levitt and Stephen J. Dubner invented. In this case, Freakonomics is a portmanteau: the blending of existing words to create a new one. But you can also modify an existing word or phrase, or create an entirely new word out of thin air.

In order for the invention of a new word to work as your main title (or in your subtitle), however, you need to do two things:

First, the word should in some way represent the new category you want to Name & Claim. If you're writing about economics, it doesn't do you very much good to invent a new word like "Shoojaku" if "Shoojaku" doesn't have the potential to own an area of expertise. Remember, you want people using this new language at dinner parties. (When *Freakonomics* first came out in 2005, people couldn't stop talking about it—and as a result, the word quickly became part of the English language.)

Be clear, not clever.

Second, the rest of the title (and the book's description) needs to articulate the POV that explains the definition of this new word. For example, the description for *Freakonomics* opens with: "Which is more dangerous, a gun or a swimming pool?" Sounds freaky! And interesting. "In Freakonomics, they explore the hidden side of... well, everything." The book's description, as well as its subtitle, provides a definition.

Giving readers a new word without a clear POV attached to it is a recipe for disaster. But if you can get it right, the word will stick—and oftentimes become part of that industry, or even the world's vocabulary.

Law #5: Use The Subtitle To Put "The Right Words In The Right Mouths"

The most effective form of marketing is, and will always be, word of mouth.

In order to spark word-of-mouth marketing, you need to put "the right words in the right mouths."

- **The Right Words** = Language that defines your category and signals your POV & leading benefit to the reader.

-

- **The Right Mouths** = Your Superconsumers (people who are obsessed with this category of thing—not just any average person on the street).

Above we used *Multipliers: How The Best Leaders Make Everyone Smarter* as an example of a book where the subtitle is, quite literally, the language the author wants readers to use when describing the book. You should be able to hear the conversation in your head just by reading the title.

"You should read the book Multipliers!"

"Really? What's it about?"

"Oh it's about how the best leaders make everyone around them smarter."

When coming up with a main title and subtitle for your book, imagine how you want people to describe your book when someone asks them what it's about. Try to pinpoint the exact words and phrases you hope they use—and then give them that language. The best place to do this is in your book's subtitle.

So your overarching template for coming up with a book title should look like this:

Big Idea Synonym: *Word-Of-Mouth Marketing Elevator Pitch*

This 1-2 punch combination of summarizing the big idea within the main title, and then using the subtitle as the "sales pitch" for why readers should care about this big idea, is everywhere. Our best-selling book analysis is littered with examples of this same template over and over again. And the times where this template falls apart is when the author (unconsciously, we assume) chooses to be clever instead of clear.

CHAPTER EIGHT

Engineering A Best-Selling Book

Checklist

We hope you found the insights in this book both interesting and actionable.

But just to make sure, we've put together a quick checklist for you here (including a few other interesting data points from our study) to help increase your chances of success as a writer, author, and industry thought leader. (We also hope publishers use this material to make more conscious decisions when helping authors refine and launch their work.)

Step 1: Choose A Top 7 Business Book Category

- Personal Development
- Personal Finance
- Insights/Thinking
- Leadership
- Case Study/Allegory
- Functional Excellence
- Relationships

Step 2: Idea-Centric vs Author-Centric

Idea-Centric books are typically more scalable than Author-Centric books because when you write an Author-Centric book, your pool of prospective readers is limited to the number of people who know who you are. Whereas anyone can write an interesting Idea-Centric book. And if the idea is compelling, new, and different, that idea can take on a life of its own—and oftentimes outgrow the author (in the best way).

Even if you are a celebrity or someone with significant social standing, if you really want your idea to "scale," it's worth finding ways to give (or at least share) the spotlight with your idea.

If the book you want to write is Idea-Centric, the categories best suited to "scale" your idea are:

- Personal Development
- Insights/Thinking
- Case Study/Allegory
- Relationships

If the book you want to write is Author-Centric, the categories best suited to "scale" your idea are:

- Personal Finance
- Leadership
- Functional Excellence

Step 3: Ascend Up The 7 Categories To A Superior Category

Regardless of which one of these mega-categories your book falls into, you want to find ways to lean toward Insights/Thinking and Personal Development to maximize both scale and pricing power. Make the content applicable and actionable to the reader's life today.

- This book will make YOU more money.
- This book will move YOU up in your career.
- This book will change YOUR habits.
- This book will change YOUR mind.

Remember: something interesting that doesn't provide any immediately applicable value to the reader is going to struggle to gain traction.

Step 4: Y Do You Write?

Once you have clarity around what category of book you want to write, and whether you are approaching that category through an Author-Centric (it's all about you) or an Idea-Centric (it's all about the idea) lens, you have to make some decisions about how you are going to execute the content and who, specifically, the book is for.

- **Is your book for beginners?** Are you solving an Obvious problem with an Obvious solution?
- **Is your book for beyond beginners?** Are you solving an Obvious problem with a Non-Obvious, surprising solution?
- **Is your book for experts?** Are you pointing out a Non-Obvious problem the reader didn't know they had, and then giving them a candy-coated, easy-to-use Obvious solution to solve this new problem they now know they have?
- **Or is your book for Superconsumers, experts, and**

hardcore enthusiasts of this particular idea/industry? Are you trying to educate them on a Non-Obvious problem they didn't know they had, and educate them on a Non-Obvious solution that requires significant understanding in order to execute? And if so: how can you give these readers a more Obvious entrypoint into your work?

Step 5: Make Your Title Best-Seller Worthy

The content of your book might be amazing, but if you whiff on the title, your idea isn't going to scale (and your book isn't going to sell any copies).

So, when coming up with your main title & subtitle, remember to follow these rules (and refer back to the formulas):

- **Rule #1:** Be clear, not clever.
- **Rule #2:** Use language that signals the primary benefit.
- **Rule #3:** The title & subtitle should mirror the Obvious & Non-Obvious pairing you've chosen.
- **Rule #4:** Use languaging in the main title.
- **Rule #5:** Use the subtitle to put "the right words in the right mouths."

Step 6: Aim For 200-300 Pages

While page count is probably the least important variable, our study showed the highest-earning business books (by aggregate sales) have an average page count in the 200-300 page range.

Step 7: Price It High

And while it's nice to have a book that moves a truckload of copies, it's exponentially different to have a book that hauls in boatloads of cash.

Our study showed there are many best-selling business books that move more copies but bring in way less money than their higher-priced counterparts. Authors who want to optimize for reach tend to price their paperback and eBooks in the $9 to $19 range, whereas **authors who make the most money from their books tend to price their work in the $19 to $35 range ($29/30 being the average).**

If you want your book to lead to a life-changing financial outcome for you and your family, then price it high.

As Category Designers, we also know that price is a seminal component to establishing value and creating differentiated experiences. "According to researchers at the Stanford Graduate School of Business and the California Institute of Technology, if a person is told he or she is tasting two different wines—and that one costs $5 and the other $45 when they are, in fact, the same wine—the part of the brain that experiences pleasure will become more active when the drinker thinks he or she is enjoying the more expensive vintage."

Keep this in mind when pricing the book you worked hard to write.

Made in United States
North Haven, CT
14 August 2022

22712935R00148